Drawing
Conclusions

Drawing Conclusions

Using Visual Thinking to Understand Complex Concepts in the Classroom

Patricia A. Dunn

TEACHERS COLLEGE PRESS

TEACHERS COLLEGE | COLUMBIA UNIVERSITY
NEW YORK AND LONDON

Published by Teachers College Press,® 1234 Amsterdam Avenue, New York, NY 10027

Library of Congress Cataloging-in-Publication Data

Names: Dunn, Patricia A., author.
Title: Drawing conclusions : using visual thinking to understand complex concepts in the classroom / Patricia A. Dunn.
Description: New York, NY : Teachers College Press, [2021] | Includes bibliographical references and index.
Identifiers: LCCN 2020044261 (print) | LCCN 2020044262 (ebook) | ISBN 9780807764923 (paperback) | ISBN 9780807764930 (hardcover) | ISBN 9780807779354 (ebook)
Subjects: LCSH: Visual learning. | Thought and thinking—Study and teaching.
Classification: LCC LB1067.5 .D86 2021 (print) | LCC LB1067.5 (ebook) | DDC 371.33/5—dc23
LC record available at https://lccn.loc.gov/2020044261
LC ebook record available at https://lccn.loc.gov/2020044262

ISBN 978-0-8077-6492-3 (paper)
ISBN 978-0-8077-6493-0 (hardcover)
ISBN 978-0-8077-7935-4 (ebook)

Printed on acid-free paper
Manufactured in the United States of America

To Kathy

Contents

Introduction

Suppose I were to ask you to visually represent two important concepts in teacher education. Suppose, for example, you had to contrast, without words, on either side of the same sheet of paper, how *formative assessment* differs from *summative assessment*, or how the phrase *emergent bilingual* has a different connotation than *English language learner*. You know these terms. Now visually represent them. Perhaps you have a knot in your stomach thinking about your dubious drawing skills (as I would). But after I tell you I don't care about the "artistic" quality of your sketches, maybe you start to think about how you might visually show the differences between two concepts. As you begin to grapple with this task, even though it may be challenging for you—maybe *because* it may be challenging for you— different parts of your brain wake up, and previously dozing neurons are engaged. What you draw, and how you write and talk about what you have drawn, may spark insights for you about these concepts. Or it might help others in your class to remember the concepts better or to understand them more deeply.

My students are mostly preservice English teachers taking courses required in our English Teacher Education program. In one of the required courses, the teaching of writing, these preservice teachers must grapple with a number of controversies: peer *response* versus peer *editing*, *code-switching* versus *code-meshing*, *formative* versus *summative* assessment, *test-prep practice* versus *authentic (real-world) writing*, and many more. When these preservice teachers are asked to quickly sketch out two concepts or controversies side by side on the same paper, their brains, first startled, must shift into high gear, all pistons firing. I call these drawings that students produce "juxtaposed visual representations" (JVRs) because there are always *two* concepts or ideas sketched next to each other, to contrast them or to demonstrate similarities and differences.

The juxtaposed concepts vary widely, depending on the curriculum of the particular teacher education course (methods, young adult literature, literacy, the teaching of writing, etc.) and also on what the individual teacher educator wishes to foreground. Some instructors might be teaching students the differences between *descriptive* versus *prescriptive* grammar, for example, or *not racist* pedagogies versus *anti-racist* pedagogies. While many

1

instructors *do* include graphics in their teaching, and scholars analyze many multimodal texts and engage students in visual rhetoric and visual literacy, most of those visual texts are produced by others. In my classes, students themselves produce the texts.

This activity, in which students visually represent two contrasting abstract concepts, promotes spontaneous thinking, which challenges and focuses thinkers immediately. They then describe in writing what they've drawn and also have the opportunity to explain it orally to the class. This process of sketching, writing, and speaking can act as a heuristic approach to spark memory, understanding, and insight, and it can promote high-level synthesis and analysis. It occasionally can function as a tool for formative assessment. Because drawing also can act as a powerful invention and organizational strategy, it is a valuable prewriting and revising tool. This strategy, meant to spark intellectual engagement, has not been studied adequately and is underused in teacher education.

WHY STUDENT-PRODUCED JUXTAPOSED VISUAL REPRESENTATIONS?

Why do I ask my students to produce JVRs of abstract concepts, ideas, or controversies important in the field and then to explain those productions? The short answer, and a mischievous one, is that the request to contrast two ideas through drawing at first befuddles them. It even can temporarily frustrate them, and me, because I always draw along with students in class. Then, after a few panicked minutes, this request to draw begins to generate thinking and rethinking. "I enjoyed drawing it," wrote one student, "though there was an initial moment of panic." First our minds struggle to imagine how we might represent abstract ideas visually, concepts that will vary, of course, depending on the specific course and what each instructor wishes to foreground.

An important idea for future writing instructors to understand, for example, is the rhetorical concept of *ethos*, the writer's credibility—both established and earned—which some believe to be one of the most important elements in successful argument and persuasion. There are two types: *situated ethos*, the reputation the writer has already established in the community they are targeting, and *invented ethos*, the credibility revealed in the writing itself, which may become either enhanced or degraded as readers work their way through the piece. Preservice teachers need to understand these two types of ethos so that they can help their students become aware of whatever positive or negative situated ethos they may hold in each rhetorical situation. Writers also need to consider how certain features of their writing (background knowledge, quality of sources, sentence variation, editing, etc.) may affect their invented ethos and thus their standing with the intended audience.

The JVRs may help preservice teachers transfer this knowledge about ethos to their own teaching. Defining a concept like invented ethos on an exam may show that the student has memorized its textbook definition. But seeing how a student has juxtaposed *situated* ethos and *invented* ethos can give a better sense of whether they truly grasp the concept. Even if the sketch itself does not explicitly address transference, the class discussion of the JVR can bring application of the concept to the fore, helping everyone see why it's important for writers to be aware of this concept and learn to make it work in their favor. The discussion this JVR sparks, coupled with seeing the images, may help preservice teachers better remember the critical role both kinds of ethos can play in argument and persuasion.

These preservice teachers may be used to explaining important concepts like these in words by referring to textbook definitions or to lectures by their professors. But to have to represent these concepts visually involves a richer, more complex understanding. They need to consider the differences between concepts on a higher level or from a different perspective. They must struggle to come up with a way to represent visually what they know. And then they must get their hands to draw objects, shapes, or symbols recognizable to others. Next, their brains must work to explain in words what they attempted to do through those sketches. In my classes, therefore, we go from reading about or discussing concepts, to visually representing them, and then back to words to explain our visuals. If we're lucky, this unexpected task sparks understanding, if not from a student's own drawing, then from someone else's when they show and explain it. This active combining of images, words, and speech—what Paulo Freire (1993) referred to as "multiple channels of communication" (p. 49)—is related to what some educators call *transmediation*, which Siegel (1995) defined as "the act of translating meanings from one sign system to another" (p. 455).

Overuse of Word-Based Pedagogies and Passive Learning

There are several longer answers to why we do this intellectual activity and to the number of problems it helps address. One problem is the overemphasis on word-based pedagogies still present in many classrooms. Information comes to students primarily through written and spoken words, and it is through words that their comprehension of this information typically is assessed. For students whose primary way of knowing is verbal, this tradition works well. For other students, however, who may explore or process information best through a *visual* approach, this relentless focus on words may be impeding their thinking or not accurately assessing what they know. Those students who explore ideas more fluently through speaking than they do through writing also could take advantage of a visual approach because of the opportunity to explain and discuss their sketches. The JVRs disrupt that word-centered tradition momentarily, allowing a wider range of learners to tap into an analytical tool they find illuminating. At the same time, those students comfortable with text-based information are productively challenged to think in another dimension. These students still get to write, also a step in this JVR process. But those who think better through speaking or sketching get to explore important concepts using their preferred symbol system, an opportunity still too rare in our schools, especially in the higher grades and in college.

The JVRs also address the hard-to-break passive learning that still dominates too many classrooms. Educators have known for decades that students need to be actively engaged in order for lasting, meaningful learning to take place. The "sit and listen" format still dominates too many classrooms, and even medical professionals warn about the physical dangers of too much sitting. When students get out of their seats to explain their JVRs projected on the screen up front and discuss their implications with classmates, that action makes it impossible, at least for several minutes, for them to be passive learners. If classes must be held remotely because of the pandemic, the JVRs still encourage active engagement. Students sketch on their own, take a photo, and show it to the class via screen sharing as they describe it.

The Picture-Superiority Effect

However, perhaps the most serious issue JVRs can help address is a widely recognized problem in teacher education: the tendency among teachers in their first teaching position to simply adopt the practices of their colleagues. This can be a good thing, of course, if these colleagues are excellent instructors who know how to respect, engage, and challenge all of their students. However, conforming to peers' teaching habits can be a problem if these new teachers adopt outdated or possibly harmful practices, abandoning student-centered, inclusive, culturally relevant, or anti-racist pedagogies that they learned in their teacher education programs. For example, instead of having their students read contemporary, diverse young adult novels written by Black or Indigenous authors, authors of color, women and men, and LBGTQ authors, new teachers might feel that they need to settle for their school's storeroom stack of 50-year-old novels, written almost exclusively by White males. Instead of responding to student writing with a mix of both specific, supportive comments as well as constructive comments, new teachers might succumb to pressure to mark every perceived error with a red pen, forgetting what they learned in college about doing an error analysis in order to prioritize editing and proofreading issues with each student writer.

Drawing, displaying, and discussing important pedagogical concepts related to those issues via JVRs in a teacher education class, however, might help mitigate the systematic forgetting and abandonment of effective practices. The multisensory aspect of this task might improve students' transference of important concepts to their future teaching. This potential to improve memory is related to what's known as the "picture-superiority effect" (Childers & Houston, 1984), that is, the tendency for people to remember information presented in images much better than information presented orally or in writing. Because the JVR process involves thinking, sketching, contrasting, writing, speaking, and listening, it taps into many of the brain's pathways, using a variety of intellectual and physical tools to help cement important concepts that preservice teachers need to retain and apply as new teachers.

Juxtaposing new ideas against old, contrasting one perspective against another, can help pinpoint our understanding of the differences between those competing ideas, concepts, or issues. In taking concepts they have read about and translating them into a visual presentation, students must focus intensely on those concepts. The act of producing contrasting sketches not only can help advance the understanding of concepts, it also can help secure them more firmly in memory because the brain is manipulating them through several channels: sight and touch when students draw the concepts, and speech and hearing when they talk about them. Writing to explain what they have drawn adds another layer. Explaining their JVRs to their classmates involves speaking, pointing, and demonstrating. In addition, listening to their classmates explain their respective drawings continues to help solidify these ideas.

These JVRs also can help us to rethink quickly how we might experiment, for example, with an alternative way of organizing a piece of writing. The resulting sketches are not artistic but holistic, tapping into different parts of the brain. Nick Sousanis, who produced his entire doctoral dissertation at Columbia University in comic book format, argues for images and words to be used together, not only to communicate, but to explore. His work, *Unflattening* (2015), was later published by Harvard University Press. Drawing, Sousanis points out, on one of his pages filled with drawings, "allows us to step outside ourselves, and tap into our visual system and our ability to see *in relation*" (p. 79, emphasis added).

Similarly, when students sketch concepts in relation to one another, their JVRs invite the altered perspective that Sousanis argues is so crucial to imagination, to fresh insights, and to higher-order thinking. By seeing ideas visually through drawing, by seeing ideas in relation to one another and simultaneously (Sousanis, 2015), we can see more. "We draw not to transcribe ideas from our heads," argues Sousanis, "but to generate them in search of greater understanding" (p. 79).

The JVRs my students draw provide the simultaneous ideas-in-relation that Sousanis describes, generate further discussion, and lead to a more solid memory of concepts and distinctions between them. The simple juxtaposed sketches students produce sometimes are able to arrest our attention in the way they "hold sequential and simultaneous modes in electric tension" (Sousanis, 2015, p. 63). We see two concepts in "electric tension." At the same time, students activate more than one mode. They write about, talk about, or listen to descriptions as they examine the two images.

Once these sketches have stopped us long enough for us to process the abstract ideas they represent, they can launch stimulating discussions and new ways of thinking about those ideas. This is especially true when several students have chosen the same abstract concepts or controversial ideas to juxtapose. No two students have ever done the same drawing, even of the same concepts. They are all different. In my classes, after students finish their juxtaposed sketches, they write a description of their drawing and then explain it to others. This multiphase activity reinforces the concepts for others. If this whole sketching process does spark visual thinking and further understanding for these future teachers, they might be more likely to try out this activity with their own students. For example, in their article on transmediation, a similar multimodal approach, Hadjioannou and Hutchinson (2014) argued that preservice teachers must experience transmediation in their teacher education programs if they are to understand it fully enough to use it as a tool in their own classrooms.

Why Two Sketches?

Throughout this book, I'll often refer to this visual representation activity as sketches or drawings. To be clear, however, they are always *student-produced, juxtaposed visual representations*. In other words, students are always drawing two side-by-side sketches of ideas that contrast in some way. The concepts, controversies, or other abstract ideas that the sketches represent are not necessarily opposites, and rarely binaries. Sometimes a concept like Universal Design for Learning (UDL) simply might be contrasted with a situation that lacks attention to UDL. These drawings are not ends in themselves, but a thinking tool for exploration and discovery. The reason to use them is not the finished sketches per se—although they can be immensely generative—but the focus and out-of-the-box thinking needed to create them. They are representations, yes, but they do not simply represent. Similar to writing-to-learn, the sketches are a form of drawing-to-learn, drawing-to-explore, and drawing-to-think. Like James Britton's (1982) classic notion of "shaping at the point of utterance"—that is, ideas emerge *as* one talks or writes—simply the *attempt* to sketch can trigger ideas. One student, Josett, wrote this about a practice sketching session we did in class: "Once I began moving the pen, the image came forward and the theme popped out for me."

In addition, sketching just one term or concept can invite people to focus simply on an accurate physical or artistic rendering and not on the important idea itself. For example, the prompt to "Visually represent prescriptive grammar" might result in a simplistic sketch of rules or a stereotype of someone concerned with grammar. But a prompt to "Visually represent prescriptive grammar versus descriptive grammar" forces the student to review those terms in their head, to seriously contemplate the differences between them, and then to make some decisions about how to represent those differences, possibly making adjustments or gaining insights during the sketching process. Two juxtaposed sketches shift the focus from a simple definition of a concept to a more discerning representation of that concept in relation to another, forcing more nuanced thinking.

Why two sketches and not one? The purpose of the juxtaposition is to examine one concept or idea in relation to another, visually, sometimes in contrast, sometimes in comparison. When I do visual representations with my classes, I always have students juxtapose two things: two concepts, two theories, two views of a controversy, two ways to organize their writing projects, and so on. (They can compare more than two if they wish.) I find that this comparison frame stimulates more mental processing than simply asking them to represent one thing. The side-by-side visual also seems to open up more discussion than does a single sketch. This constructed side-by-side visualization forces people to think and to grapple more deeply with the implications of whatever concepts are being drawn and discussed. Explaining their JVRs, both in writing and orally, pushes them even further, as does listening to classmates explain their always-different renderings of the same concepts. Having visual images of these concepts also will help students remember them, and why they are important, longer.

Why two sketches and not three or four? There are several practical reasons. First, most of my preservice English teachers, like me, find any sketching fairly difficult. Juxtaposing two representations requires the contrastive thinking I'm trying to get them to do. Adding a third or a fourth would be too overwhelming a task for the 10 minutes or so I allow for this exercise in class, and it might shift too much attention to how to squeeze all these ideas on one sheet of paper. Also, since we discuss a number of these in class after the sketching is done, three or four sketches on one page would be difficult for all of us to see. On the other hand, discussing just two sketches projected side by side on the screen brings the focus back to the important ideas being contrasted in relation to each other.

The craft or skill involved in these two juxtaposed drawings is immaterial. The act of drawing, the cognitive effort it takes to generate even a simple sketch of abstractions, is in itself an intellectual engagement with complex ideas. It's an invention tool, a point of departure for discussion, a way to review or remember material, a clue to students' understanding of concepts or issues. The act itself is an enzyme to learning.

ADVANTAGES OF JUXTAPOSED VISUAL REPRESENTATIONS

My instinct as a teacher told me visual representations were doing something worthwhile: graphically illustrating important concepts, generating discussions, and making connections with issues related to teaching writing. Research in a number of disciplines is beginning to reveal why and how images spark these intellectual processes. As mentioned above, one well-documented advantage to using visuals is the picture-superiority effect (Childers & Houston, 1984): People remember images more easily than they remember words. The New London Group's (1996) work on multimodality and visual design has been highly influential. They argued for pedagogies to include more of what they called "multiliteracies," an umbrella term that includes cultural, technological, visual, and other multimodal approaches. That group also recommended that pedagogies employ a "multiplicity of communication channels," echoing Paulo Freire's (1993) earlier call for educators to employ "multiple channels of communication" both in their teaching and in what students composed.

Science and Visuals

The STEM fields, of course, rely on visuals to communicate their findings to readers. In Lynda Walsh's prize-winning *Written Communication* article, "Visual Invention and the Composition of Scientific Research Graphics" (2017), she summarizes the results of her study, in which she surveyed 144 STEM researchers regarding their invention processes for designing and including graphics in their work. A common practice among them, she discovered, was the use of comparison. In fact, many of Walsh's participants used contrast and comparison in their graphics "to demonstrate the novelty of results" in their experiments (p. 25). This use of comparison and contrast in these STEM researchers' graphics in order to emphasize their findings may suggest why my students' juxtaposing of contrasting concepts or different sides of a controversy so often yields visual representations that spark discussion or insight. Perhaps it is the stark side-by-side contrast, graphically visible on the same page, that enables viewers to instantly engage with complex ideas. In our visual system, as Nick Sousanis (2015) has explained, it is the parallax, the space between our eyes, that allows us to see from two slightly different perspectives at once, providing depth perception. Similarly, students' JVRs sometimes can spark a richer perception of concepts.

Active, Multimodal Learning

The title of this book, *Drawing Conclusions*, emphasizes the action of drawing these juxtaposed concepts, for example, *active learning* versus *passive learning*, or *standards* versus *learning objectives*, or whatever abstract

concepts a teacher educator wishes to explore further. When students visually represent these or other concepts, the drawings, along with the explanations that accompany them, help all of us to delve more deeply into the
concepts and discuss their implications. The book title also refers to the
conclusions students inevitably draw regarding these concepts. Therefore,
these *student-produced, juxtaposed visual representations* can also reveal
the extent to which students truly understand the concepts they have drawn,
although assessment is never the primary reason for doing this intellectual
exercise. In fact, most of the sketches we do—and we do only two to four
per semester—are done quickly in class so that we can view and discuss a
few of them, and these are not assessed at all. We do them for the intellectual stimulation they provide and the insights they can reveal about the
concepts we're studying at the moment.

I've been having students produce sketches like these in my classes for
a long time. This current project, in which I analyze drawings students produced in five classes over the course of three semesters, is a greatly expanded
follow-up to and broadening of the "sketching-to-learn" sections from my
book, *Talking, Sketching, Moving: Multiple Literacies in the Teaching of
Writing* (2001), and from my co-written *Kairos* article, "Reversing Notions
of Disability and Accommodation" (Dunn & De Mers, 2002). As I acknowl-
edged in the 2001 book (p. 66), I owe to a former student, Kathy Iannone,
the initial idea to have students contrast different paper organization plans.

Kathy was a preservice teacher with a background in art who was an
observer and teaching assistant in a 1st-year writing class I taught at Utica
College in upstate New York in the early 1990s. At that time, in that class,
my students were having trouble organizing a long research project. They
had completed initial drafts, but the thought of organizing these drafts
seemed overwhelming to them. I tried to help as best I could, but I had
about 75 first-year writers, plus a literature class, so my time was greatly
divided. Therefore, we had students sketch out their existing organizational
pattern and contrast it to a possible alternative one. Then they showed their
two patterns to the class and discussed them, which in turn helped other
writers see alternative patterns for their own projects. Ever since then, I've
used that exercise to help students with long writing projects rethink how
they might better organize their drafts.

Since contrasting sketches were so useful to help students reorganize
their papers, I started to experiment with using students' juxtaposed visual
representations in other situations that seemed to call for a stepping-back,
a distanced view, a different perspective. I've used a version of that sketching exercise to help students grapple not just with writing projects but
with concepts and controversies they're reading about in classes I teach in
our English Teacher Education program: writing and rhetoric classes for
preservice English teachers, adolescent literature, English education methods classes, graduate classes in composition theory, research, linguistics,

rhetoric, disability studies, and literature. The student sketches published in *Talking, Sketching, Moving* came from classes I taught at Illinois State University, when I had Institutional Review Board (IRB) permission, and students' permission, to do so. I've continued having students do these contrasted drawings since I came to SUNY Stony Brook in 2003, and they have generated many good discussions and learning opportunities. For years I've wanted to stop and analyze the products of this intellectual activity. But other projects intervened, and only recently have I pursued and secured IRB permission for such a project centered on visual representation. Not since *Talking, Sketching, Moving*, however, have I stepped back this far to analyze the drawings after the class has ended, to sort them as I have here, and to realize how much they could teach us.

Analyzing the JVRs

I must confess that sometimes I did not fully comprehend the insights some of my students expressed through these juxtaposed visual representations until I had this time to study them more closely and read the students' explanations more carefully for this project. I frequently told my students not to think of these sketches as "art," mostly because I didn't want to cause anxiety among people like myself who cannot draw as well as the least artistic kindergartner. I also wanted them to focus on ideas and concepts, not quibble with craft. However, like some of the best art, many of these sketches, when analyzed in more depth, yielded rich connections or points of departure I missed during class discussions of them.

The same was true for some of the explanations accompanying the sketches. When going through the artifacts I had collected, and reading students' descriptions of their work, I sometimes saw something I wish we had pulled out and discussed even further in class, or something that told me the student had misunderstood something I thought everyone learned in the beginning of class. This analysis, therefore, has turned out to be valuable in its own right and also helpful in planning how I'll use JVRs in future classes. Using JVRs is not a substitute for other ways of accessing, processing, or assessing knowledge. But they can be a valuable supplementary tool, one that can reveal aspects and implications of abstract concepts that might be missed through word-based methods alone.

I am deeply grateful to those students who graciously produced sketches in these English classes (where they didn't expect to have to do so) and then gave me their permission to use their drawings, their descriptions of them, and their opinions about them collected in surveys. I respect their intellectual curiosity in taking this odd classwork seriously and following me down this path, still relatively untrodden in teacher education and in English studies. This project would not have been possible without my students' generosity and trust.

The Chapters

In this book, different chapters feature different JVRs, all of which juxtapose concepts whose hidden assumptions have critical implications for teaching.

Chapter 1 explains step by step how I scaffolded activities to prepare students to draw these visual representations of abstract concepts or important controversies. In this chapter, I also explain how one of the examples can be used to show preservice teachers how the interpretive stance they choose in discussing literary texts may affect the extent to which their classrooms are inclusive and respectful—or not—of all groups in their class.

Chapter 2 provides examples, explanations, and commentary on visual representations produced by some of my students on the following concepts related to literacy or to the teaching of writing: different kinds of teacher or peer commentary, school writing versus authentic (real-world) writing, and other issues critical for preservice teachers to not only understand but apply. Since several of these samples revealed students using drama, pathos, and perspective shifts in their drawings to illustrate a literacy-related concept or take a position on a controversy, this exercise increases the chance that students will remember these issues and how they affect pedagogical choices. These sketches help us see how policy-induced drama and emotion might play out in classrooms, even if the drawings are peopled just by stick figures. The visuals, coupled with the emotion evident in them, can help to further cement important concepts related to the teaching of writing, accessible documents for users with disabilities, and inclusion.

Some visual representations revealed that students did not fully understand some important concepts from class, including one concept especially important regarding issues of diversity and cultural assumptions about students' language practices. In Chapter 3, I show samples of these latter types, explaining how they were an eye-opener for me and a useful formative assessment tool. Discussing these JVRs also acted as a gentle corrective to misconceptions others in the class might have had.

Samples in Chapter 4 are from a graduate class I taught on how to teach literature, especially on how the critical/interpretive lens used would greatly impact what texts were taught, how they were approached, and what impact texts and discussions about them might have on real people.

Juxtaposing current and possible alternative organizational patterns is a quick way for writers to consider major reorganization of drafts, or to experiment with solutions to problems they see in their developing drafts. Students whose visual representations appear in Chapter 5 contrasted a current organizational structure with an alternative one. Sometimes they juxtaposed a problem they had in their current draft to how they might solve it. The sketches themselves, or sometimes the class discussions of projected samples, were quite helpful for some students as they reconceptualized possible revisions of their major writing projects.

Chapter 6 summarizes results of a short survey given to participants, asking them to what extent they thought sketching juxtaposed concepts was helpful to them regarding increasing understanding of material or providing insights about organizing their major writing projects. I provide a quantitative summary of the scales they filled out, along with some selected comments (both pro and con to this visual thinking activity). I also discuss the limits of this research, changes I would make in a future iteration of such a study, and further recommendations for teacher educators who wish to adapt the best parts of this thinking.

We want our preservice teachers to do more than just define terms and concepts related to how they teach their future classes. We want them to have a deep understanding of how their choices will affect their students' engagement, self-esteem, confidence, and learning. The books these teachers select, how they discuss them, what writing or other projects they design, how they respond to students' work, what assumptions they make about their students—all these factors need to be discussed, argued about, and reflected upon. Having students create juxtaposed visual representations of some of these critical concepts can promote this clarification and reflection. In Chapter 1, I provide a detailed explanation of how I scaffold the process of getting students to produce these JVRs, and I show some examples and how we use them.

Preparing to Juxtapose Visual Representations

How and when do students produce visual representations in my classes? How do I scaffold activities to prepare students to do them? What do we do with them once they exist? First, it's important to note that there's a fine line between giving students enough preparation to feel comfortable trying these drawings and giving them so much information that they overthink the task or try to imitate an example I've shown them. While I do not wish to cause unnecessary anxiety in students who, like myself, consider themselves terrible artists, an element of surprise gets students' attention and breaks them out of business-as-usual thinking. When I ask them to sketch in class, I want them to feel that they are in a safe space, that the activity is low-risk, and that we're doing it for the sake of the intellectual activity itself, not for the resulting product. For those reasons, I'll often model the process. That is, I'll sketch something casually on the board to explain something on a day when I am not going to ask them to draw. Sometimes I'll do a juxtaposed sketch; sometimes I'll simply sketch to explain something.

MODELING THE PROCESS

To illustrate this point, I've included a sketch I did in a class on teaching literature to show students my rendition of *new criticism* versus *poststructuralist approaches* such as feminism, queer theory, critical race theory, postcolonialism, reader response, and disability studies (see Figure 1.1).

This JVR is meant to graphically illustrate how an interpretive stance or a particular critical lens can have real-life implications regarding inclusionary or exclusionary teaching. I explain that on the new criticism side, no one is analyzing the analysis going on. The students simply are putting the text at the center of attention, as if that is the default mode of what one does with a text in academia. The text is larger and much higher than they are. No human agent is visible who might have placed this text at the center of attention. It is simply there, as if it has always been. And if, for example, a canonical novel represents in a stereotypical way characters

Figure 1.1. New Criticism Versus Poststructuralist Approaches

Two juxtaposed scenes, with stick figures. On the left, labeled "New Criticism," a text sits atop a kind of trophy or fancy goblet, which in turns sits atop a desk. Surrounding the desk, and way below the top of it, three stick figures look up at the text, their arms raised, as if in adoration. No teacher is visible. The text is at the center. On the right, labeled "Poststructuralism," a teacher stands with a text in hand, pen raised, as if taking notes, observing the students. The five students are each interacting with a text in a different way. The texts are as big as they are. One stands on top of the book, hands raised as if in victory. Another simply stands on top of the text. Three students each lie underneath giant texts, as if crushed by the texts.

with whom some students in class identify (who may be students of color, or young women, or students with disabilities, or LGBTQ students), the interpretive approach may be focused on plot structure or theme or literary elements, but not on the problematic representation. Texts that students cannot identify with, or texts that may be disrespectful in their character-ization of some groups of people, sometimes are allowed to be featured year after year, in class after class, because with their obvious metaphors and abundant literary elements, they lend themselves nicely to the kind of new critical interpretation still demanded on many old-fashioned, high-stakes assessment essays.

Texts and Interpretive Lenses

On the poststructuralist side of this JVR, though, the critically conscious teacher is observing the text's apparent effect on each student and taking notes, reflecting on what she sees. Some students are empowered by what they're reading; thus they stand, triumphantly, on top of the text. These might be texts with which these readers identify, or the setting and conflicts might be similar to those they face in their lives. Perhaps the protagonists in these texts look like them or live in cultures like theirs. The story being told in this text reminds them that people like them are worthy of having their stories told and discussed in classrooms everywhere. The other students, who are being crushed by the texts, may be feeling disempowered by the text being foregrounded in this class. Perhaps the stories of people like themselves are not represented in the text, or in any text read so far in school. Or perhaps the characters in the text who *are* like them are disrespected in some way by the other characters or by the situation. Perhaps a character with a disability is depicted as pitiable (Tiny Tim in *A Christmas Carol* or Laura in *The Glass Menagerie*) or as dangerous (Lennie in *Of Mice and Men*). What's worse, perhaps this disrespect goes unnoticed and unremarked upon, not only by the other characters in the text, but by the questions being posed about the text regarding its themes and symbols. The questions posed about a text and the discussions about it are engendered by the interpretive or critical approach used by the teacher (or by the textbook author). And these discussions, in turn, can make students feel included or excluded in their English classes, perhaps causing them to love or hate reading or school in general. That is why it's important for preservice teachers not only to define the technical differences between these approaches to literature, but to grasp the assumptions that underpin these approaches and therefore the classroom practices that spring from them, which can be inclusionary or exclusionary.

In my JVR, I was attempting to show that most poststructuralist approaches do not center the text in the way new criticism does. Poststructuralism and other, more recent theoretical frameworks are more likely to pose questions about the role the text plays in either challenging or reinforcing stereotypes about women, people of color, LGBTQ people, people with disabilities, and so on. Poststructuralism also can promote "close reading," as does new criticism, but the purpose of the analysis is not necessarily to understand or applaud the text itself but to understand the text's context and role in the world—and perhaps to question that role. In the sketch on the right, the teacher is not looking at the text, but at the students and their reactions to the text. As I'm looking at my own sketch now, I wonder why I didn't have the teacher replacing the oppressive texts that were crushing some of her students, or giving the satisfied students a text that would take them out of their comfort zones for once. Maybe the next time I draw this in class, I'll have two panels on the poststructuralist side to show the teacher doing more than simply noticing her students' reactions. I also might add another figure to the new criticism side, perhaps having one student glancing toward the poststructuralist side, peeking through the panel, also noticing the different effects of these texts on students. What I like about this sketch, if I do say so myself, is that it gives us a thumbnail way to discuss a wide range of interpretive and critical approaches to literary texts. Examples like this one, which I sometimes sketch live on the board as students watch, demonstrate the drawing-as-thinking process I am going through as I explain something. It also shows them the level of technical craft that's needed (not much) for the type of visual representations I'll eventually ask them to do. As one student I had had in a previous class remarked drolly as I was assuring students in a subsequent class that they did not need to be artists, "The bar is not very high."

I'm careful not to scaffold the process too much, however, because I don't want students to think they need to emulate my primitive stick figures in their own drawings or even use stick figures at all. I list as many options as I can think of for these drawings: geometric shapes, objects (as metaphors), concentric circles, graphs, charts, and so on, and students are free to come up with their own approaches. I want them to know just enough about what we'll be doing so that they don't freak out, but to be (pleasantly) surprised enough to just start doing it without a lot of models to follow. The less they can picture these sketches ahead of time, the more variety there is in what students produce and the more imaginative the sketches are.

Scaffolding the Intellectual Tasks Needed

Before we do juxtaposed visual representations as a class, I also scaffold some of the intellectual tasks involved: grappling with course readings, making connections between those readings and class activities, identifying important concepts in education, and considering how those concepts might play out in a real class that these students will teach in the future. For these reasons, I don't ask students to draw during the first few weeks of the semester. I want students first to get to know one another, to wade a bit into the course material, and to trust me enough to try the sometimes unusual activities I design for the class.

To help prepare students for the drawing that will come later, I ask them to do several written responses to the readings early on in the semester. In these relatively short (500-word) essays, I ask students to summarize two or more of the readings so far, to pick out possible controversies, to make connections between those readings, and to compose an open-ended question appropriate for high-level class discussion. Then in class we address some of the questions they posed. A few weeks later, I ask students to do a 2-minute audio response to class readings, also making connections, identifying concepts, and designing an open-ended question. Doing a verbal, recorded response to the readings, something most of them have not been asked to do before, throws them a gentle curve. It introduces them to the idea of playing with ideas in a mode different from writing. While most students are used to speaking during class discussions, it is extremely rare for students to get a full 2 minutes of uninterrupted time to comment on course material. Most students simply send me a 2-minute audio file. Occasionally someone will call my voice mail to do the audio report, and once in a great while, a student will come to my office and deliver their comments in person. Like the written response to the readings, the audio response invites students to engage with course material again, summarizing and making connections. Because the audio response is somewhat novel, students are initially a little nervous about doing it. But everyone completes the assignment, and I'm diligent about letting them discuss the experience afterward and about using in class the questions they posed in their audio reports. Once students have had some practice revisiting course material through written responses, and survived doing the unconventional audio responses, we can begin experimenting with juxtaposed visual responses in class.

For these juxtaposed visual representations, students are to contrast, on the same sheet of paper or screen, two related but somewhat opposing ideas or concepts. In a language class, for example, they might represent *prescriptive* versus *descriptive* grammar, *code-switching* versus *code-meshing*, and so on. In a class on the teaching of writing, they might contrast written commentary versus audio commentary, or conventional writing assignments versus real-world (authentic) writing.

Students typically do these sketches two or three times during the semester, once or twice in class, as practice and to generate discussion, and then once on their own, at home, as part of a reading response project that will be a small portion of their final grade. The ones we do in class are not graded at all; they are done to get us thinking, discussing, and reflecting further on the contrasted ideas. I assign one low-stakes reading response that they do at home via a juxtaposed visual representation, once we've done several in class. I assign this out-of-class piece mostly so that they can take their time to draw it, more time than I can devote to it in class. It will count as only 5% of the class grade, and I assess it very generously. I grade this project mostly so that students take this thinking tool seriously. No one has ever received a low grade on it. In future classes, I may not assess these home-produced sketches at all, if I'm convinced students will take the task seriously enough to devote some time to it at home.

Here is how this project is explained on my syllabus:

Reading Response #3 is a *visual representation* that juxtaposes two related but conflicting concepts related to the teaching of writing.

Artistic talent is not necessary, but knowledge of concepts is. Imagination helps. We will practice this in class before you try this at home. You will explain your visual representation to a small or large group of classmates (and me) and also explain it in writing. More directions and criteria TBA.

Note: Much writing in school is done in response to texts. These responses are designed to have you experience multimodal ways of responding to texts—as invention or drafting strategies. Think about how modifications of these different intellectual tasks could be used as invention strategies for your students.

Much more detailed directions are given later in the semester.

Practicing and First Attempts

Here's a typical example of how these sketches happen. I'll ask students to take out a sheet of paper, or sometimes I'll simply distribute plain copy paper. I ask them to think about an issue, concept, or controversy related to the readings or course discussions so far, and I start by naming some myself, to model the process. Then students chime in with some suggestions, adding to the possibilities. These issues vary from course to course, but there are always a number of competing theories or concepts to review or interrogate further. I tell them to fold the paper in half, demonstrating it myself, and to draw a line along the crease going down the middle.

On that divided sheet, I ask them to juxtapose, in a visual representation, two abstract issues we've read about so far in class. Facing many stunned, even panicked looks, I explain that this task is not to be thought of in any way as "art," but as a way to wake up some dozing neurons in their brains, to help them discover some new insights, and to maybe generate a useful original metaphor. I assure them that no one expects a detailed, sophisticated rendering from this quick in-class activity. Those who have seen my previous drawings are less nervous about this task. They can use stick figures (as I often do), geometric shapes, rough graphs, pie charts, simple cartoons, sketches of objects, animals, trees, roads, and so on. After we've brainstormed some ideas, and I lower their stress level as best as I can, I give them 10 to 15 minutes of class time to produce their practice visual representations. I always do one too during this allotted time. I also ask them to write several sentences explaining their sketch, and I say that they'll have an opportunity to show it to the class, but only if they want to.

Once my own sketch is decent enough to show to the class, I take a photo of it on my tablet. Then I walk around the room, stopping at the desks of those who look finished, and I ask whether I can take a photo on my tablet to show to the class. Some say yes; some say they'd rather not. Once I have five or six visual representations to display, I turn on the projector and plug in my tablet. Some students are just finishing up, which is fine, but since many are now just jotting down their explanations, I begin to show the slides. Because my drawings are pretty primitive (think untalented kindergartner level), I usually go first in order to show them they need not be afraid that their sketches are too simple. I also explain my sketch orally, since there's no way it would be clear on its own. This way, I can model the process, standing at the front of the room and pointing to the different sketches on each side, explaining what the figures are supposed to be, and what abstract concepts are being juxtaposed. Inevitably, my stance on the concept or controversy is fairly evident in the sketch.

After I've shown my sketch and explained it, I move on to a student's sketch, displaying it on the screen for all to see, and ask that student to explain it. Some students come up to the front of the room and point, like I did, and some stay in their seats to describe what's on the screen. Although this project was completed before our university's COVID-related switch to remote learning, this activity easily could be adapted to video conference platforms that allow screen-sharing. In fact, an online class session would make it even easier for students to show their JVRs and to be heard when they then explain the sketches.

Many of the sketches are, understandably, not terribly inventive or interesting, given the time limit and the newness of this in-class task, and I thank the student politely and move on quickly to the next. Some leave me speechless, not because they're good, but because they demonstrate that the student has completely misunderstood an important theory or concept we've been studying in class, or because they completely disagree with me about some practice I've recommended (see Chapter 3). Some of these sketches, however, are brilliant, perfectly crystallizing an important controversy, raising a critical question, or inventing an insightful metaphor. These rare but provocative visual representations are often humorous, or almost breathtaking in how they so starkly capture the essence of a controversy. They can generate much discussion and engagement, helping us review a concept or further clarify it for everyone.

DEEPENING DISCUSSIONS

How do I use these sketches to launch deeper discussions of important issues? Let's say, in a class for preservice teachers on the teaching of writing, we are reading about Joseph Williams's (1981) *phenomenology of error*, a concept important for people who are going to be future teachers and instructors of writing because it can affect their initial perception of a student's writing as well as how they assess that writing. Here is how this phenomenon works: When people are reading a piece of writing done by someone who they expect to make errors, such as a student, those readers tend to find a number of errors, even if some of the "errors" might be simply stylistic differences from what the reader would have written. In contrast, if a person is reading work by a high-status writer, say, a Pulitzer Prize–winning author, a renowned professor of English, or even an honors student known as an excellent writer, that reader does not expect to find mistakes and likely will read right over all but the most egregious errors that might be in the text. This different perception of error based on the reader's expectation is a version of confirmation bias, what Williams calls the phenomenology of error, which he demonstrated in his academic article by embedding some errors that he rightly predicted few people would notice.

The phenomenology of error is a bit more complicated and also is related to the rhetorical concept of *ethos*, which can greatly affect the persuasiveness of a piece of writing. If the writer has a strong, positive reputation or ethos in their community (situated ethos), their argument will be received more positively than if they have a reputation as unreliable, unprincipled, or foolish (Crowley & Hawhee, 1998). As readers continue through a piece of writing, the writer's invented ethos can increase or decrease in the reader's mind, based on elements such as sentence structure, quality of evidence, tone, and so forth.

It's important for future writing teachers to be aware of these effects so that they can attempt to be as fair as possible when reading their future students' papers. Or, since full objectivity is so difficult to obtain, savvy teachers who know about the phenomenology of error may try to grade their students' papers without knowing who wrote what, thus mitigating some of the prejudging that this phenomenon no doubt causes. Reading Williams's essay is one way that future teachers can learn about this concept, and discussing his essay and its implications is another. A visual representation, however, can cement the idea more efficiently and more dramatically. Because all writers can benefit when they become consciously aware of the phenomenology of error (for it can make them more alert to readers' preconceived notions of them as writers), it's important for these future teachers to remember this concept so that they can teach it to their own students. Visual representation can help students understand and remember this concept. I was pleased, therefore, when one of my students represented that concept visually.

Student's JVR Provides Insights

In a graduate class on theories and practices of teaching writing, during one of our practice sessions, Jackson juxtaposed clever cartoon panels to explain Joseph Williams's concept of the phenomenology of error. (Most students' names in this book are pseudonyms, except for a few of the students who wanted their real first names used.) In my classes on the teaching of writing, I want these current students and future instructors to be well aware of how

Figure 1.2. Jackson's JVR Showing the Effects of Joseph Williams's Phenomenology of Error

Two juxtaposed cartoon panels, one above the other. In the top panel, a professor, wearing a tie, is smiling as he gives an "A+++" to a paper. A thought bubble over his head shows the professor is imagining a scholarly-looking writer: a man wearing a suit jacket, bow tie, and elbow pads, and smoking a pipe. He also carries a briefcase. The bottom panel shows the same professor, not smiling, who is giving an "F" to a paper, on which he has circled several things, drawn arrows, and written in the margins. In the professor's thought bubble is a young man wearing a sideways baseball cap and a chain, carrying a cell phone, and smoking a cigarette.

both ethos and the phenomenology of error can affect students and teachers alike. Figure 1.2 shows Jackson's sketch and his explanation of his depiction of the phenomenology of error. He shows the same instructor, grading the exact same paper, but imagining two different students as authors of it.

Here is how Jackson describes it:

> The drawing (hopefully) illustrates the phenomenology of error—how preconceived notions can influence grading. When the teacher believes the paper is written by a scholar, he does not see errors. When he believes the writer is a problemed student, he grades more harshly.
>
> I chose this concept because the binary seemed clear. I enjoyed drawing it (though there was an initial moment of panic) and thought about how I could add distinguishing features and embellishments to make it clear that it was the teacher's assumptions and not the paper itself that was different.

Like some of the other concepts we discuss in this graduate class on the teaching of writing (such as not marking every error on a student's paper, having students write in a variety of genres aimed outside the classroom, seeing "clarity" as a function of both the writing and the background knowledge of the reader), the phenomenology of error is a concept that goes against the grain of conventional views of error. It seems counterintuitive for many students new to composition studies. They may be thinking, "Error is error, right? It doesn't matter who makes it. Readers can be objective and treat all writing the same, regardless of who wrote it."

We know, however, that writing instructors, being human, are subject to having the same preconceived notions as other humans, and that they may be affected by those assumptions. I always teach students about the phenomenology of error, therefore, to help them to name and be wary of this very human tendency. I want them to think twice about how they may be grading and to occasionally experiment with grading papers without names on them, or at least to be conscious that they might be making prejudicial assumptions. Jackson's sketch, in which students can see the exact same paper getting wildly different grades because of who the professor thinks wrote it, could be immensely helpful in explaining this concept.

This sketch, with the professor's apparently negative assumptions about a "problemed" student, also would be an opportunity to discuss gender, class, ability, or racial stereotypes, and how they play into assessments of writing. The male professor in the sketch pictures one writer as a "scholar" and gives the paper an "A+++." He pictures the other as a young man, possibly a student of color, and gives the same essay a bright red "F." How might the professor's assumptions about those two writers affect the "errors" he notices in the essay? As Young et al. document in their book *Other People's English* (2014), vernacular, code-meshed statements made by students of color are often not tolerated by their English teachers, yet some White, professional writers frequently use code-meshing in their writing, which is paid for and published in major news outlets. Although this cartoon foregrounds the phenomenology of error, it also opens the door to productive connections with diversity issues (race, gender, class, disability) related to teaching and assessment of writing. The recent #DisruptTexts movement on Twitter, at the National Council of Teachers of English, and elsewhere, begun by Tricia Ebarvia, Kim N. Parker, Lorena German, and Julia E. Torres (n.d.), asks preservice and practicing teachers to examine their assumptions and biases and how they inevitably affect how teachers treat their students of color. A JVR that shows how a teacher makes assumptions about students and then grades on those assumptions would be a good way to open conversations that could interrogate teachers' assessment practices.

Summary of Preparation for JVRs

To sum up this process, I end this first chapter with a quick review of how I prepare my preservice teachers to engage with this often highly stimulating intellectual activity. While there is no one way to introduce and prepare students to experiment with juxtaposed visual representations in order to enhance their understanding and insight, here is a brief outline of how I scaffold activities leading up to the sketches we do in my classes. The JVRs featured throughout this book were all produced following this basic pattern.

- I identify important ideas, abstract concepts, or controversies critical to the course being taught. (In my classes, I've used descriptive versus prescriptive grammar, standard English versus standardized English, canonical texts versus contemporary graphic novels, and many more, but each instructor will have their own ideas of what's important in their classes.)
- I make sure students are used to making connections between readings and are able to identify important concepts on their own. I do this through structured written and oral reading responses, where I ask specific questions about connections, concepts, and controversies.
- After students have a chance to get to know the instructor and one another, and after they've gone through several rounds of connecting with course material via conventional reading responses, I take some time in class to do a visual representation myself.
- To model the process, I go up to the board, draw a vertical line down the middle, and sketch out a very simple representation of two opposing concepts or ideas. Sometimes I draw it ahead of time and project it in class, but I prefer to do it "live," so students see

that I'm not looking for artwork but just a representation we can talk about. Sometimes I think of ideas to juxtapose before I go into the class; sometimes I think of things at the spur of the moment.

- Once I show students my humble sketches, I ask them to try their hand at it. The first time I ask them to draw, I provide the concepts I'd like to have them juxtapose.
- I give them 10–15 minutes of class time to do these sketches. I sketch at the same time.
- Using my tablet, I take a photo of my sketch.
- I usually ask students to write a short paragraph explaining their sketch. (Otherwise, some of them are indecipherable, as are mine without at least an oral explanation.)
- Then I walk around the room with my tablet, looking at their sketches, seeing who is finished, and asking students whether I can show their work to the class via projection. Some say yes, so I take photos to project them.
- I usually project mine first, to reduce students' anxiety about showing their sketches, most of which turn out to be much better than mine. I explain what my sketches are supposed to represent, and then I talk about what the sketches mean and what I am trying to do.
- Then I ask one of the students whose drawings I photographed to get up and explain their projected visual representation. Often that brief explanation leads to a clarifying, deep discussion of the concepts they chose.
- I ask a few more students to explain their sketches. Projecting and discussing three to six student sketches can take anywhere from 15 minutes to a half-hour—longer if some of the discussions are particularly insightful. Adding in the time it takes for students to sketch during class time, therefore, instructors would need at least a half hour of class time to do this activity. Forty-five minutes or an hour is better.
- After the class has done this activity once or twice during the semester, it is time for students to juxtapose visual representations as a response to class readings on their own time. When those are submitted, I ask a few students whether we can view and discuss in class what they produced.
- These steps can be easily adapted to remote synchronous or asynchronous teaching.

The remaining chapters in this book foreground some JVRs my students produced. Some show dramatic scenes that can help viewers better imagine the real-life consequences that education policies or concepts can have on students, making teaching either more inclusive or more discriminatory.

Some JVRs instantly clarify differences in abstract concepts in ways that will help us all remember the concepts better. Some JVRs showed me how some students did not fully understand a concept, and some helped students reorganize their substantial writing project for that semester.

The student-produced JVRs included in this book demonstrate how JVRs can promote intellectual engagement with abstract concepts and controversies critical to course content. They tap into the power of metaphor and visual adjacency to increase exploration, understanding, and perhaps transference and memory.

JVRs are powerful intellectual tools because they:

- employ active learning and scaffold pedagogical strategies (Chapter 1).
- demonstrate the roles that drama, pathos, and perspective shifts can play in understanding and persuasion (Chapter 2).
- act as a low-stakes but important formative assessment tool (Chapter 3).
- help students grapple with complex literary and critical theories (Chapter 4).
- aid in reorganizing and revising a long writing project (Chapter 5).
- are a strategy many students find helpful (Chapter 6).

It's my hope that those who read this book will begin to experiment with having their own students produce juxtaposed visual representations. This heuristic is still relatively new to teacher education, one that will work in different ways in different contexts. I will continue to use JVRs in all of my classes to see what insights they have yet to offer. This book, however, showcases some of the most interesting snapshots of this process, as well as some reflection on and analysis of what happened.

CHAPTER 2

Pathos, Perspective Shifts, and Metaphors

As research across the disciplines has demonstrated, visuals can act as a learning tool that encourages diverse and inclusive approaches to thinking. Because student-produced JVRs both invite and allow students to process ideas using multiple modalities (sketching, writing, speaking), more students get to think using an intellectual path that is most generative for them. In addition, more students are productively challenged to try an intellectual pathway, such as drawing, that conventional pedagogies underuse as a resource, especially in high school or college English classes. The process of thinking about how to represent an abstract concept, plus the effort it takes to render that idea on paper, is valuable in itself because it forces students to revisit the concept, perhaps read about it again, and consider how it compares with a competing idea or practice. Then they must play with ideas on how to represent these different, sometimes opposite ideas in a visual format, through visual metaphors, charts, geometric shapes, perspective shifts, and so on. Everyone has to think hard, but they do so in a safe, low-risk environment.

Once students have produced these sketches, usually after a 10-minute in-class practice session, I project several of them, with their creators' permission, of course. Some of these JVRs can be both persuasive and memorable because of the drama they display, for example, when students use stick figures. Showing what can happen when these little beings encounter obstacles in their education can draw in viewers instantly. It is immediate, visual, and dramatic. Unlike many academic articles, these sketched scenes also can provide instant perspective shifts. We can read about controversies related to our course content: how much teachers should "correct" students' writing, the pros and cons of rubrics, the effects of deficit thinking—or whatever ideas warrant discussion in a particular course. However, seeing an issue, such as a teacher's overcorrection of student writing, play out, dramatically, in an almost storyboard format, can bring the problem to the foreground more vividly through characters' internal or external conflicts, thought bubbles, and dialogue. These techniques can evoke sympathy. When we view such juxtaposed panels, we are there in the moment, seeing two perspectives on the same page. We are drawn into a scene where a powerless student may be experiencing injustice, perhaps because of a new (or old) policy or a curriculum decision—or lack of one. We see the educational issues we've been reading about play out in front of us and affect these students, even if they're just cartoon figures.

Not every student-produced JVR is provocative or dramatic in this way. However, each time we do a round of these side-by-side panels, several of them illustrate a way of thinking about an issue that teaches us all something or makes us think more deeply. This is because stick figures, if used in students' JVRs, represent people. Their simple smiles or sad faces immediately can demonstrate the emotional consequences of employing, or not employing, a controversial practice or approach we've been studying in a methods or literacy course. While possible emotional effects on students can be described in a written piece, a juxtaposed visual representation of a person experiencing an emotion can be seen instantly and perhaps can be retained longer and play a stronger role in persuasion.

PATHOS, DRAMA, AND STICK FIGURES

School and college instructors spend much time responding to student papers, so it's important that preservice teachers become familiar with research on this much-studied issue, critical to students' development as writers as well as their attitudes toward writing. The JVR shown in Figure 2.1 took up teacher commentary on students' writing: what works, what does not, and what student writers find most helpful. This sketch, which features emotion, was drawn during a 10-minute impromptu segment of class time. The sketch reframes an idea we read about and discussed in my class: whether and to what extent teachers "correcting" every error on students' papers is helpful to those writers.

For example, in her summary of previous studies on how students react to teacher commentary, Nancy Mack (2013) pointed out that praise is the "first and foremost" ingredient instructors must include, in balance with specific, constructive comments, in order for their responses to be useful to students (p. 248): "In summary, teacher commentary is most effective when it relies on specific praise with a few, brief statements about options for specific improvements" (p. 249). Mack's advice echoes Donald Daiker's earlier recommendations in "Learning to Praise" (1989), his comprehensive overview of dozens of teacher commentary studies spanning decades of research back to the 1960s, including Paul B. Diederich's (1963) important work on the benefits of praise, which both scholars pointed out is sorely lacking in many instructors' responses to students' papers. A litany of what the student is doing wrong not only results in overload for writers, but it also can discourage them from future writing. In fact, focusing too much on traditional

Figure 2.1. Caitlin's JVR Contrasting the Imagined Effect of Overcorrection With the More Likely One

Two scenes juxtaposed on a sheet of paper. On the left side, a smiling stick figure teacher holding a "trusty red pen" has made multiple markings on a student's paper, with "vague" and question marks and other markings visible. In a thought bubble, she is thinking, "I'm going to be so helpful to my students and let them know all the areas where they can improve!" On the right side, a student with bags under his eyes is holding up the same marked-up paper. His thought bubble says, "Just got my essay back . . . I might as well not try. I can't do anything right!" [Note: the printed lines seen bleeding through from the other side of the paper are the result of her having used some scrap paper to do this sketch.]

school "grammar" in general is not a recommended practice for improving writing. As George Hillocks Jr. wrote in a famous meta-analysis he did in 1984:

> In some studies a heavy emphasis on mechanics and usage (e.g., marking every error) results in significant losses in overall quality [of writing]. School boards, administrators, and teachers who impose the systematic study of traditional school grammar on their students over lengthy periods of time in the name of teaching writing do them a gross disservice that should not be tolerated by anyone concerned with the effective teaching of good writing. (p. 160)

In contrast, telling writers what works and pointing specifically to what they are doing well not only encourages reluctant writers, but also lets them know what, specifically, to keep doing in future papers. In their study of how 2-year college developmental writers reacted to teacher commentary, Carolyn Calhoon-Dillahunt and Dodie Forrest (2013) found that many students preferred the "end comment" on their papers because it "may be one of the most important places on the page for them to receive affirmation that their ideas were heard and considered, perhaps even influencing their continued growth as academic writers beyond the paper they attempted to revise" (p. 242).

In a recent study, Anson and Anson (2017) found that while there is still a need for ongoing faculty development regarding commentary on student writing, there has been some progress recently, with instructors focusing more on "preferred practices" that address idea development and other "higher-order" rhetorical and structural issues instead of commenting just on "lower-order" concerns such as grammar (p. 12). In my classes on the teaching of writing, therefore, we spend a lot of time studying this research and practicing responses to works-in-progress.

Different Perspectives on Teacher Commentary

The visual representation of the different sides of this issue in Caitlin's cartoon in Figure 2.1 amplifies the effect, in a way that a word-based article might not do, of a teacher's overly exuberant correcting and editing of a student's essay. The use of *pathos* as a rhetorical strategy, more vivid in a sketch, also may influence an audience. The JVR illustrates the following problem: With perhaps the best of intentions, a teacher can mark up students' papers, pointing out and fixing all perceived errors in hopes of helping students avoid such errors in the future. But students are sometimes overwhelmed and discouraged by all those red-inked corrections, so the teacher's good intentions and substantial time investment in markups can have an effect opposite to the one hoped for.

Caitlin describes her sketch this way: "Too much feedback/copyediting can be overwhelming to the student, even though the teacher may have the best intentions." It's possible that a word-only explanation of this situation might be sufficient to help readers understand how a teacher's intentions in correcting a paper might clash with the effect these corrections might have on the student. However, Caitlin's juxtaposed sketches emphasize the stark contrast between two people's different perceptions of the markings on this paper. The teacher, holding her "trusty red pen" and smiling with satisfaction, sincerely thinks all her corrections now on the student's paper will help that student in the future. The student on the receiving end of those comments, however, with bags under his eyes and a slightly turned-down mouth, is discouraged by all the markups. His thought bubble says: "Just got my essay back . . . I might as well not try. I can't do anything right!" This depiction is consistent with multiple studies on teacher commentary, dating back decades, that show how the impact of negative feedback outweighs that of positive comments on students' papers and also how students typically react to that feedback (e.g., Daiker, 1989; Diederich, 1963). In spite of fairly consistent findings regarding what students *do* find helpful (specific balanced feedback, both positive and constructive, and feedback given over time, not all at once, etc.), many instructors still feel obligated to mark every departure from what they deem to be correct.

Caitlin's cartoon adds a visual element to this clash in teacher commentary practice, thus helping to deliver the message via several pathways. As mentioned earlier, the picture-superiority effect (Childers & Houston, 1984) may account for why Caitlin's cartoon may draw attention to this issue in a way that plain sentences cannot. People also may retain knowledge better if they can associate it with a visual image. This simple cartoon may do a better job than print in promoting Caitlin's implied argument about the danger of "too much feedback/copyediting."

Another important element in Caitlin's sketch is *pathos*, a powerful rhetorical tool that taps into our emotions, making the conflict or issue more vivid and real. In their well-known textbook, *Ancient Rhetorics for Contemporary Students*, rhetoricians Sharon Crowley and Deborah Hawhee (1998) pointed out, citing Cicero, that appeals to emotion—pathos—can be as powerful as logic and ethos in argument. Pathos can move people when facts may not. When we are drawn into a scene where, for example, a young character is experiencing emotional distress, we are more likely to be moved, and then persuaded, by the rhetor's efforts. The name for this rhetorical device is *enargeia*, "a figure in which rhetors picture events so vividly that they seem actually to be taking place before the audience" (p. 155). If we can visualize the emotional toll an event has on a character, it can "stimulate similar emotions" in us. To illustrate enargeia, Crowley and Hawhee pointed to the famous speech Marc Antony gives in Shakespeare's *Julius Caesar*, all the while holding up Caesar's bloody garment for the crowd to see. As we know, that powerful demonstration, filled with pathos, completely reverses the crowd's view of Caesar's death.

The stick figure dismayed by all the red-inked corrections on his paper is not Shakespearean drama, but Caitlin's little scene also employs a form of enargeia, a visual scene that can be described in words, but here can be seen instantly in the sketch. These contrasted scenes help us "picture events" in a way that an essay warning about the dangers of overcorrection might not. The emotional effect of seeing the distressed student—the pathos in the situation—also may help convince viewers to rethink their teaching practice if they are themselves too addicted to their red pen. Reading research that documents the possible harm heavy markups can do is one way to obtain information. Seeing a cartoon where an individual suffers may not only cement the information but change people's minds about the still-widespread practice of error overcorrection. Granted, written texts can and do include appeals to emotion. In the cartoon version, however, we see the student's sad, tired expression, and his reaction is now written in first-person narration: "Just got my essay back . . . I might as well not try. I can't do anything right!" This peek into a student's thoughts has an immediacy, drama, and pathetic appeal sometimes lost in a word-only version.

Access, Inclusivity, and Diversity

Another cartoon from the same class and same sketching practice session also uses emotion to illustrate an important topic from the class. This one, drawn by Alexa (Figure 2.2), makes an implicit argument about the importance of using alt text (alternative text or image description) to describe images for readers who cannot see the page or screen but are using a screen reader that will read the description of the image aloud to them—but only if the creator of the text has added such a description in the code. In my class, which teaches future teachers how to teach writing, I try to emphasize the importance of having accessible teaching materials, with alt text being

Figure 2.2. Alexa's JVR Contrasting Inclusive Versus Noninclusive Images

Juxtaposed scenes regarding alt text (alternative text). In the left frame, labeled "Inclusive," there is an image of a dog on a computer screen. The image has an image description: "The photo shows a brown dog with his tongue sticking out." Five stick figures stand around the photo. One person says, "I see!" Another person, wearing sunglasses, says, "I see it, too!" All figures are smiling. On the right of the page, labeled "Not Inclusive," is a photo on a computer with three people playing with a ball. There is no alt text. There are four smiling stick figures. One of them says, "We see!" The figure with the sunglasses has a sad face. He says, "I can't see." This cartoon has been drawn on lined paper. The student wrote her description on the other side of the paper, and her writing bleeds through a bit.

an easy and basic requirement for accessible texts. Many people still do not know how to add alt text. In fact, many of my students say they have never heard of it.

Alexa's sketch, like Caitlin's, also revisited an important point we had read about and discussed in class. Also like Caitlin's, Alexa's sketch somehow makes the case for using alt text more immediate, dramatic, and emotional. Here is her written description: "Using alt text in photos helps those who cannot physically see get a good idea of what everyone else is looking at. Without it, the blind remain blind, and cannot interact with the material."

Like Caitlin's visual representation of teachers' corrections discussed above, Alexa also uses stick figures to illustrate a point. It's one thing to read a written guideline to "Use alt text for images." But seeing the situation from the perspective of a blind person—even a stick figure—who feels left out because they cannot see an image may be more persuasive to those who don't often think about alt text or the reason for it. The drama in this little scene enables us to see the effects on one individual who cannot participate to the same extent as their classmates. Again, there is a visual element of pathos here. An essay can plead with readers to use alt text. A cartoon figure experiencing distress can demonstrate why they should. The use of human figures, the drama of exclusion, and the frustration of the student who cannot see the image may all combine to impress on the class, in a way a sentence cannot, the importance of using alt text.

Seeing information through different modalities also can help bring new realizations. It wasn't until I wrote this section that I noticed something about Alexa's cartoon: In order for the blind person to be aware of the alt text description, they'd have to be using a screen reader, which would read aloud to them the description of the image, if an alt text had been provided. Standing around looking at the screen would show them neither the photo nor the description of it. The alt text, of course, would be a description delivered auditorily through the student's screen-reading software. If I had noticed that detail when Alexa was explaining her sketch to the class, I might have reminded students about how screen readers work (although it may have embarrassed Alexa). I also should have reminded students first that the teacher should have described the image orally to the class, a basic accessibility guideline for showing slides to a group.

However, Alexa's overall point in these juxtaposed images about the importance of alt text is well taken, in spite of the flaw in depiction. Because of the pathos involving the blind student, the message about using this inclusive tool might be cemented in viewers more strongly than it might be in readers merely reading a word-only directive to do so. The stick figure is happy in the left panel, where alt text includes them in the lesson. Their sad face in the right panel shows them hurt at being forgotten. Although just a stick figure, its down-turned mouth can help us see, in a way print text may not, the emotional toll noninclusive practices can have on an individual.

Emotion in Ancient Rhetoric

Sharon Crowley, in her book *Toward a Civil Discourse* (2006), reminded us that the ancient rhetoricians knew that to truly sway an audience, rhetors needed to use much more than simply logic and facts. Drawing on Barbara Herrnstein Smith (1997), Crowley argued further that rhetors should rely less on logic and reason for persuasion, and more on "the arousal of passion and desire," which are emotions (p. 195). It is emotion, Crowley argued, that is one of the "primary motivators" in getting people to believe something or to act (p. 59). This view, of course, runs counter to how argument currently is taught in schools, where most instruction insists largely on "facts" and students pointing to "evidence from the text." As the sketches in Figure 2.2, with their use of pathos, demonstrate, however, we may be moved by these images to think about inclusivity, diversity, and access for disability more often, and sooner, when we are preparing slides or other teaching materials that include images that should be described for readers who are blind or visually impaired.

Issues of race, class, gender, and disability also are embedded in linguistics, a required course for most preservice English teachers. One issue involves students for whom English is not their first or home language. A related linguistic concept we study, both in my teaching of writing classes and in my history of language class, is how people accommodate, or refuse to accommodate, differences in language and accent. Drawing on social linguistics, Rosina Lippi-Green (2012) explained what she called the "communicative burden," which represents the difficulty speakers face when they do not know each other's language. Lippi-Green pointed out that most times in Western culture, it is the learner of English who is tasked with carrying more weight when two people are trying to communicate. This uneven distribution of effort puts too much responsibility on one person, and not enough on the other. It can result in bad feelings on both sides, not to mention a barrier to communication for both.

Metaphor and pathos in juxtaposed scenes also play a convincing role in the sketch by Jackson, shown in Figure 2.3, regarding the communicative burden. Here, using moving a couch as an analogy everyone can understand, Jackson shows what can happen when people either angrily reject, or happily embrace, the communicative burden. Jackson's juxtaposed scenes encapsulate Lippi-Green's concept. But they do more. Using drama and pathos, Jackson argues implicitly through this representation that both parties will be happier, and the couch will be safer, if they cooperate and share the communicative task.

Figure 2.3. Jackson's Contrasted Scenes of Rejecting, Versus Accepting, the Communicative Burden

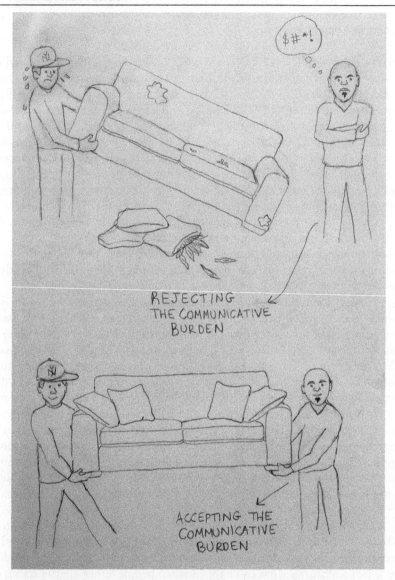

Two juxtaposed scenes, one above the other. The top one, labeled "Rejecting the Communicative Burden," shows two men, one in a baseball cap, beads of sweat dripping from his head, and clearly unhappy as he tries to lift a couch by himself. The other man, standing with his hands folded and curse words in his thought bubble, refuses to help. The couch here is torn, with holes in it, and couch cushions lie on the floor, their stuffing coming out. The bottom scene, labeled "Accepting the Communicative Burden," shows both men, smiling, lifting the couch and sharing the weight. The couch is intact.

Here is Jackson's explanation of his juxtaposed scenes:

One of the subjects we've discussed in this class is the communicative burden and how it disproportionately falls on ELLs and those who speak with an accent. As Lippi-Green notes in *English with an Accent* (2012), misunderstandings often result from or reflect the attitude of the Standard American English (SAE) speaker, rather than any genuine difficulty in hearing or comprehending: "In many cases, however, breakdown of communication is due not so much to accent as it is to negative social evaluation of the accent in question, and a rejection of the communicative burden" (p. 73). In my illustration, rejecting the communicative burden is analogous to not helping your roommate move the couch into your new place. Undue stress is put on your roommate and the couch ends up scuffed, torn, and worse for the wear, even if you do eventually manage to get it up to your apartment—to this end I've tried to show that the accent-speaker (in the baseball cap) is sweating and that the standard English speaker (bald guy) is frustrated. Accepting the communicative burden/ accommodative behavior is, like helping your roommate with that couch, more equitable, effective, and pleasing to both parties.

The couch is a perfect metaphor for "carrying the weight" of the communicative burden. The couch dragging on the floor versus the couch being safely conveyed would have been enough to provide an instant visual snapshot of the communicative burden concept. Jackson, however, adds emotion to this snapshot. The two men in the top sketch are clearly distressed—the lifter sweating and unhappy, the stubborn non-lifter cursing to himself. The two men in the bottom sketch, now sharing the weight and burden of the couch, are no longer sweating and cursing. They are both smiling. So the cartoonist clearly is implying that everyone can benefit from a more cooperative attitude about dividing the labor of trying to talk with one another. All parties gain something. What's more, these juxtaposed visuals suggest that this more evenly divided communication strategy also benefits society. One-sided labor results not only in negative emotions on both sides, but in a damaged couch (communication). Shared labor pleases both parties, and it keeps the furniture safe (and the communication more pleasant and effective).

We see, then, that juxtaposed visual representations can add dramatic human elements to theories or practices students have read about. Drawn fairly quickly, JVRs sometimes add emotion to contrasting scenes, demonstrating how concepts in education play out in classrooms and affect individual students, enlivening discussion and promoting further thinking. The contrasted scenes possible in these sketches have the potential to generate empathy, provide viewers with an alternative point of view, and perhaps open or even change minds.

Scientific Research on Emotion

The pathos or emotions revealed in these students' juxtaposed visual representations may be more significant than we initially might have believed, given the simplicity of the sketches and the speed with which some of them are produced. The ancient rhetoricians credited by Crowley and Hawhee (1998) with recognizing pathos, enargeia, and the role emotions play as a powerful enzyme in persuasion knew what scientists confirmed many centuries later. As Crowley noted in *Toward a Civil Discourse* (2006), since the early 1990s neurologist Antonio R. Damasio and his colleagues (1996) have been studying the role that emotions and feelings may play in how people make good decisions. This phenomenon is not limited simply to the emotions and feelings we are aware of as we make large or small decisions. Research focused on what Damasio called "the somatic marker hypothesis" suggests that the prefrontal cortex of the brain, a region that processes emotions and feelings, can affect decisionmaking, even when people are not consciously aware of that process or of the emotions triggered in that region of the brain. He found that some subjects who had damage in that region of the brain, but whose logic, intellect, and retention of factual knowledge were unaffected, had difficulty making life decisions such as making plans, choosing friends, or even organizing their day. In his laboratory research, Damasio found a way to study these changes directly. This research, as described in a scientific journal aimed at neurobiologists, is too detailed to summarize properly here. But it is consistent with more recent findings about the role emotions play in human decisionmaking and may account for why JVRs have so much potential for both learning and persuasion.

Attitudes Revealed in Sketched Images

What's particularly fascinating about Damasio's findings on emotions, however, is that emotions can operate on an unconscious level, affecting our decisions without our conscious awareness that they are doing so. "While the hidden machinery underneath has been activated, we may never know it" (Damasio et al., 1996, p. 1416). This research is also relevant here partly because it suggests that images can play a role in helping knowledge become "minded," that is, made conscious. I cannot say, of course, that Damasio's neuroscientific findings about emotions, feelings, and images relate directly to the pathos and emotions depicted in these students' sketches. But his research suggests that they might.

Simple stick figures expressing joy or pain might well play a role in revealing to the cartoonist how they feel, deep in their unconscious prefrontal cortex, about a debate or concept related to language, teaching, or reading. The resulting sketch also might tap into decisionmaking on the part of viewers, affecting their perspective on the issue. In an activity designed to tap into students' deep feelings about different varieties of English, April Baker-Bell (2020) had her students draw images to represent their views of what she calls Black English and White Mainstream English. Citing previous literacy research (Albers et al., 2013; Kirkland & Jackson, 2008), Baker-Bell demonstrated how these images "helped me get underneath their language attitudes where their perceptions of their cultural, racial, and intellectual identities in the face of anti-blackness and white linguistic and cultural hegemony were buried" (p. 43).

As Crowley (2006) noted, when ancient rhetoricians instructed their pupils about the powerful role pathos could play in persuasion, they predated by many centuries today's "research in neuroscience and cognitive psychology" (p. 82), especially neuroscientists' somatic marker hypothesis and their study of the role emotions and feeling play in decisionmaking. Citing the views of two cognitive psychologists (Clore & Gasper, 2000), Crowley pointed to the strong role emotions can play in what we pay attention to and what we believe: "The relative intensity of an emotional response can either alter or reinforce belief" (p. 83). The ancient rhetoricians were, and contemporary scientists are, on to something we should study further. The attention to pathos in these sketches might help us begin to do that.

This summary of attention to emotions in disciplines across the curriculum is just a small sampling of published work on these topics. It does establish, however, the importance of these elements to cognition, to learning, to making connections, and to rhetorical argument and persuasion. The research in these different academic areas concerning visual imagery, perspective, and thinking contributes to an understanding of why having students produce visual representations can be so valuable.

PERSPECTIVE SHIFTS

In addition to being able to quickly evoke empathy and pathos, these side-by-side sketches instantly can represent more than one side of a controversy because they simultaneously can show a radical shift in perspective, with the images quickly doing the work it might take paragraphs to describe. Occasionally, students who know something about comic art are able to visually represent intellectual or even physical shifts in perspective that quickly illuminate an issue in education. These JVRs can show the crux of an issue, not in a long academic article, but in a couple of seconds.

One sketch that makes its point through a physical perspective shift is Erin's, shown in Figure 2.4. Her topic emerged from discussions we'd been having about students being allowed to use or barred from using cell phones and laptops in class, and the implications for students who needed them for accessibility purposes. Many educators have heard colleagues debate this issue in faculty meetings. Some are rightly concerned with distractions

Figure 2.4. Erin's JVR Showing a Revelatory Shift in Perspective

Two juxtaposed cartoon panels. In the first (left) panel, two stick figure students, a boy and a girl, sit on a park bench reading on their cell phones. In the background, other people seem to be wailing and fainting, with a cityscape behind them on fire. Another person, this one with hands raised to head, is thinking, "Kids these days and their phones are DESTROYING THE WORLD!!!" In the right panel, the cartoon is labeled "On their screens." The perspective has shifted, and now we are behind the two students on the bench, and we can see what's on their cell phone screens. The boy's screen shows a long to do list, with "Brainstorming for my FanFiction!" at the top. The girl's screen shows a Google search for "scholarship opportunities," with 67435 results.

caused by students' non-course-related scrolling, texting, or even shopping on their devices when the devices are allowed in class. However, for instructors familiar with discussions about the role that laptops and other devices play in the lives of students with disabilities, there is no debate: Devices should be allowed in class. Furthermore, individuals should not need to "out themselves" as having a disability if they need these devices to take notes, to access course materials electronically, to read course materials in an accessible format (making the print larger, for example), or as a way to help them pay attention. As Jay Dolmage argued in *Academic Ableism* (2017), when teachers do not allow laptops in their classes, they "force students for whom the use of a laptop is an accommodation to be clearly singled out" (p. 91). While there are challenges in allowing all students to use their devices in class, these problems are outweighed by the need for students to have the technology they require in order to learn best, whether they carry an official "disabled" label or not. Erin's JVR, a comic, takes up an issue related to the controversy surrounding young people and technology: adults' disapproval of young people focused on their cell phones.

Here's what Erin wrote about her juxtaposed visual representations, labeled "Technology/Phones/Social Media":

> On one side, two youngsters sit on a bench on their cell phones.
> Behind them, the city appears to be burning, people are in
> distress, and someone yells: "Kids these days and their phones are
> DESTROYING THE WORLD!!!". On the other side, we see the
> screens of their phones, where they are doing creative and practical
> things (brainstorming for a creative writing project, and researching
> scholarship opportunities).

When I asked students to reflect a bit on what they did, Erin wrote:

> When I set off to draw this, I had this model image in mind of a
> political cartoon. I wanted to use hyperbole in the first image (city
> burning, etc.) because to millennials and now Gen Z, that's how
> ridiculous some of those criticisms feel to us. Drawing this was not
> only fun but it got my gears going, and I feel like it can be a great way
> to frame the two sides of an argument. It also forces some specificity in
> panel 2 (i.e., coming up with something to be on their screens).

Erin's point-of-view shift in these panels makes her argument. First we see the students and the overaggravated and fainting adults from a distance. We cannot see what the students are doing on their devices. In the right panel, we are now behind the students and can see what they actually are doing on their devices: researching scholarship opportunities, generating creative projects, and so on. This perspective shift allows viewers to see for themselves how wrong the adults in the first panel are to assume the two young people are "destroying the world" because they're looking at their cell phones. It's a simple yet insightful way of literally looking at a situation from a 180-degree physical perspective shift.

What's more, Erin's explanation provided me with another insight about genre. In this class, we had been talking a lot about having students write in different genres: letters to the editor, film reviews, sets of directions, blogs, and so on. In just about 10 minutes, Erin produced yet another genre available to students, the political cartoon: brief, strong arguments that work best without a lot of words. The images do most of the heavy lifting, but they require viewers to actively put the pieces together to get the point.

When a sentence or an image requires readers or viewers to actively participate in drawing a conclusion, the situation is similar to the classic rhetorical device *enthymeme*, which Sharon Crowley (2006) described as "a rhetorical deductive argument" (p. 206). It works, and is made stronger, by having the audience draw conclusions based on the premises in their head. Crowley drew on Aristotle's concept of the enthymeme to demonstrate how visual images can work. She wrote that the Greek root word for enthymeme is *thumo*, or viscera:

> Words, performances, images, and other representations appeal to the gut. They trigger emotional responses that can set off a chain of ideologic that can in turn arouse additional emotional response. The resulting affect may seem to under-write the empirical truth of whatever conclusion is drawn. (pp. 87–88)

What's most interesting, and perhaps most convincing, about enthyme-mes and enthymemic visuals is that people must "work out other premises and make the desired connections. Their participation in the construction of the argument may even create a kind of visceral satisfaction for the audience, thus closing the circle of acceptance" (Crowley, 2006, p. 88). In other words, people are not simply reading or seeing passively. They must participate actively in making the connections in their own minds between the informa-tion provided and what is implied, thus making those connections stronger.

Erin's JVR requires viewers to participate in drawing this conclusion: The adults collapsing on the sidewalk or holding their heads in frustration over young people's cell phone use are wrong. The sketch is not a classic enthymeme, but it persuades using a similar technique of forcing the audi-ence to finish the logic chain. I agree with Erin that a political cartoon "can be a great way to frame the two sides of an argument," even as it reveals the cartoonist's opinion on the matter and persuades viewers to agree with them. Furthermore, the task of creating the JVR also functioned for Erin as an invention strategy, a tool for generating ideas: "Drawing this was not only fun but it got my gears going." While her finished sketch turned out to be illustrative and, I believe, persuasive, the action of producing the sketch was valuable for Erin for its own sake because it got her thinking.

METAPHORS

Some of these JVRs are simply visual ways to illustrate teaching of writing practices we're reading about and discussing in class (effective teacher com-mentary on students' papers, the use of laptops in class, making teaching materials accessible for students with disabilities, etc.). Others synthesize and represent, in a visual way, contrasting pedagogies or theories related to language or learning.

Another topic frequently discussed in my teaching of writing class is the difference between *prescriptive* grammarians and those who consider themselves *descriptivists*. To explain this briefly and no doubt reductively: Prescriptivists resist language change, quote old grammar rules, and try to prescribe what they see as a stable, "correct" use of words. Descriptivists, on the other hand, recognize that languages and rules change over time, and that we can describe what seems to be "correct" usage, but descriptivists also understand that "correctness" is always a function of time, context, purpose, and audience. Space prohibits a more nuanced discussion of those two terms, but future English and writing instructors need to think about the implications of those two categories and how their own view of language and language change will affect their pedagogy.

In my class we read several essays from *Garner's Modern English Usage* (2009) because Bryan Garner uses a lively, humorous prose to explain these different views of language. In an essay at the beginning of the third edition of his book, he has an essay entitled "The Ongoing Struggles of Garlic-Hangers." The "garlic-hangers" in the title refers to a quote Garner credited to linguist John McWhorter (2008), who made fun of language guardians he saw as clinging to rules that had already changed, comparing radical prescriptivists to superstitious citizens from the Middle Ages: "All attention paid to [linguistic prescriptions] is like medievals hanging garlic in their doorways to ward off evil spirits" (McWhorter, 2008, as cited in Garner, 2009, p. lvii). When this topic comes up in class, I draw a continuum on the board, with "prescriptivist" on one end of the line and "descriptivist" at the other end. I place myself on the line where I think I best fit, not at either extreme, explaining that my place on the line (and my view of language change) is not always consistent. Then I invite students to think about where they would place themselves on this continuum.

We need not be completely on one side or the other, of course. I'm not trying to be nosy or to pin them down. But I do want these preservice or currently practicing writing teachers to be aware of these almost diametrically opposed categories and to think through the implications of each perspective. Do they see themselves as gatekeepers, slamming the door on the "irregardless" users of the world? Or do they welcome new words and changing usages of them? Does their view of language change depend on the circumstances in which the change is happening—where the new word or new usage originates? What roles do race, gender, age, disability, and social class play in their assumptions about "grammar," "correctness," and language change? These are critical questions because teachers' views of language greatly affect their judgments of their students and their students' language use. How they communicate with their students about language is deeply connected to issues of inclusivity, social justice, and diversity. I was pleased, therefore, when a student tackled this issue of prescriptivism versus descriptivism in a powerful visual metaphor, giving us a chance to discuss it further. Figure 2.5 presents another JVR by Jackson, submitted as a reading response project. The two "sides" are juxtaposed.

Here is Jackson's explanation, which has the title "Visual Representation: Prescriptivist vs. Descriptivist":

> My illustration depicts the difference between prescriptivists and descriptivists, as discussed in *Garner's Modern English Usage*. Prescriptivists are sticklers for traditional rules of grammar and meaning, trying to preserve the "sacred cow" of standard English. Their efforts are mostly in vain because semantic change is inevitable, as unstoppable as an oncoming train. Descriptivists recognize this inevitability and see it as their job to describe and catalogue these changes, hence the camera, regardless of their potentially negative effects on language, writing, and the culture at large (lack of clarity, loss of meaning, lowering of standards, etc.). The garlic hanging around the prescriptivist's neck is a nod to Bryan Garner's reference to garlic-hangers, "conservatives in matters of language" (p. lix, quoting Baugh & Cable, 2002, p. 336).

Jackson's cartoon is useful because "modern usage" as the "unstoppable train" of language change is such a powerful metaphor. From a different perspective, coupled with a strong metaphor, we can see instantly the foolishness of the person trying to stop that train by pushing against it with his body. The descriptivist, however, uses a camera with which "to describe and catalogue these changes." These cartoon images—of a prescriptivist trying to stop a moving train, and a descriptivist photographing it for curating purposes—not only may help viewers understand and remember these differences. The visual representation also can be used to open up debate about language change. The new, changed uses of "irregardless" and "literal" are not popular with a lot of English teachers, and now here they are in this cartoon, riding merrily along on the train that no one is stopping. It's fairly clear where the cartoonist stands on this issue, yet he has left some room for people to debate it. After all, the speeding train smashes the cow to pieces, with "Standard English" thrown up in the air. We might have done much more with this metaphor had we had more time, perhaps adding ourselves to the panels in some way or mapping onto them some of the scholars we had been reading about who had various positions about language change. Jackson's extended metaphor of the speeding train opened the door to that kind of discussion.

Metaphors have a powerful influence on our thinking. Metaphors, of course, use objects we can see to represent abstract ideas we cannot see: a heart for love, a tree for life, a dove for peace, a train for language change, and so on. That's partly why these JVRs are so useful. Often employing metaphor, they can make visual—for a moment—abstract ideas new teachers

Figure 2.5. Jackson's JVR Contrasting Prescriptivist and Descriptivist Views of Language Change

Two juxtaposed cartoon images, one above the other: the top one labeled "Prescriptivist," the bottom labeled "Descriptivist." In the top, "Prescriptivist" panel, a man with glasses and a tie is pushing back on a train called "Modern Usage," trying to stop the train from hitting a cow labeled "Standard English," which is standing on the railroad tracks. The man is wearing garlic around his neck. The cow has different words on different parts of its body: "disinterested," "regardless," "literal," and "peruse," along with several punctuation marks (exclamation point, question mark, semicolon). The "Descriptivist" panel on the bottom also has the same Modern Usage train, but this train has words on it like "irregardless" and "literal," as well as those punctuation marks. The same man is in this panel, but he is not wearing the garlic around his neck or attempting to stop the train. Instead, he holds a camera and is snapping a photograph of the train.

must not only understand but grapple with when they make decisions regarding their curriculum, teaching materials, course design, and so forth.

The study of metaphor and its effect on us is both current and interdisciplinary. Recent work in linguistics regarding theory of metaphor and metaphor analysis has shown that the thinking involved in how humans process metaphor is complex. People use a variety of cognitive processes involving "cross-domain mappings," "compression," "integration networks," and "double-scope blending" (Fauconnier & Turner, 2008). Too complex to detail here, these cognitive processes surrounding metaphor make this figure of speech "one particularly important and salient manifestation of conceptual integration" (p. 53). Metaphor, wrote Fauconnier and Turner, "often drives key aspects of art, science, religion, and technology" (p. 53).

Amy Cook and Seth Frey (2019) used "metaphor theory" (p. 189) and "cognitive metaphor studies" (p. 191) tools to help readers appreciate Shakespeare's poetry and use of metaphor. Cognitive linguistics emphasizes "embodiment" as a way to examine Shakespeare's metaphors (p. 190). This theory is part of cognitive studies. Cook and Frey explained: "Cognitive dynamics is an umbrella term covering dynamic varieties of cognitive psychology, psycholinguistics, and cognitive linguistics—all within cognitive science" (p. 196). They also pointed out that Lakoff and Johnson are "the initiators of cognitive metaphor studies" (p. 193). In their well-known book, *Metaphors We Live by* (1980), Lakoff and Johnson wrote, "Most of our fundamental concepts are organized in terms of one or more spatialization metaphors" (p. 17). As those authors pointed out, "Metaphors are part of our conceptual system"; yet that system "is not something we are normally aware of" (p. 3). Like the pathos and enargeia exhibited in the sketches shown earlier in this chapter, metaphors can work stealthily, influencing our thinking and our view of the world without us being consciously aware that they are doing so, thus increasing the lasting effect of the images in which they appear.

Visualizing Varieties of English

The prescriptive/descriptive grammar standoff that Jackson represented in his train metaphor is but one of many language issues related to power, prejudice, and oppression. As numerous scholars have pointed out (Gilyard, 2000; Smitherman, 2012; Young et al., 2014), our attitudes about language cannot be separated from our assumptions about race and standard English. Likewise, the prescriptive/descriptive grammar debate cannot be separated from related issues of social justice and which English language varieties are promoted or discouraged in schools. The controversy surrounding what sometimes is called "Black English" has been one of the most longstanding and contentious issues related to what gets taught in English classes. As Toni Cade Bambara (1974) commented on this subject almost a half-century ago:

In short, there is an active and productive camp whose position is that the mono-linguistic-mono-cultural fanaticism that has reigned supreme in the classroom must cease. And that Black English must be encouraged in the curriculum for it makes, simply, good pedagogical sense to produce content, present material, encourage learning in its patterns. (p. 105)

Almost 50 years later, this subject is still controversial, still not solved. In her book *Linguistic Justice: Black Language, Literacy, Identity, and Pedagogy* (2020), April Baker-Bell uses the phrase "Anti-Black Linguistic Racism" to describe "the linguistic violence, persecution, dehumanization, and marginalization that Black language-speakers experience in schools and in everyday life" (p. 11). It's important, therefore, that preservice teachers understand and discuss language through these opposed views of language variety and change.

Related to debates regarding language is the current one surrounding *code-meshing* and how it differs from *code-switching*, another issue we read about in my course, Studies in Language and Linguistics. One of the texts we read was Vershawn Ashanti Young et al.'s *Other People's English: Code-Meshing, Code-Switching, and African American Literacy* (2014), in which the authors outline what they see as critical differences between code-switching and code-meshing. Code-switching, according to Young et al., involves teaching students "to switch from one code or dialect to another, that is, to switch from using African American English to Standard English, according to setting and audience" (p. 2). The authors describe code-meshing as the blending of "African American language styles together with Standard English at school and at work" (p. 1). Young et al. argue that code-switching can set up or perpetuate a hierarchy. It can promote inequality and discrimination regarding language use because the message behind the advice to switch can be interpreted as students' home languages being perceived as "not good enough" for school or work. In contrast, code-meshing, the authors argue, can encourage a more egalitarian view of all versions of English. In the book, the authors also give examples of how this code-meshing-informed pedagogy might be implemented.

This topic is complicated and fraught with all of our preconceived and often racist notions about groups of people and what versions of language are "proper" or "appropriate." This issue is also difficult to explain quickly because there are different definitions and opinions about the two concepts, as well as a mix of research results. (For deeper background and contrasting or different views of related issues, see Canagarajah, 2006; Guerra, 2012; LeMoine, 2001; Smitherman, 2012; Wheeler & Swords, 2006.) Code-meshing, and the related issue of standardized English, struck a chord with my students. Several of them took it up in their visual representations, using metaphors and enabling us to revisit points brought up in our class readings and discuss implications of these two approaches.

Ella's juxtaposed visual representation, shown in Figure 2.6, is an excellent point of departure to begin discussions of these issues, to review them, to debate them, or to see how they might manifest in society. She uses everyday objects, a pedestal and a construction level, as visual metaphors to represent different varieties of English.

Figure 2.6. Ella's JVR on Different Varieties of English

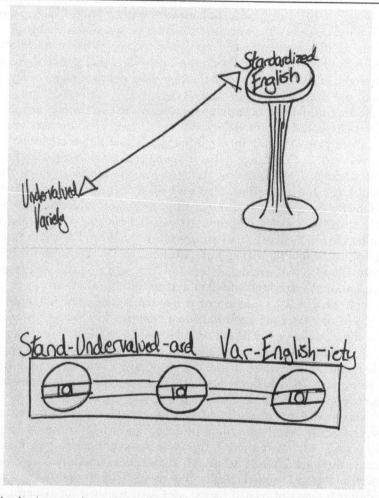

Two sketches juxtaposed, one on top of the other. In the top sketch, the words "Standardized English" sit atop a pedestal. A two-way arrow points down to the left corner, where sit the words "Undervalued Variety" way below the pedestal. The bottom sketch depicts a large construction level, with the bubbles in the level centered. On top of the level is the made-up long phrase, "Stand-Undervalued-ard Var-English-iety."

Here is Ella's explanation of her sketches, which she entitles, "On a Pedestal vs. on the Same Level: A Visualization of Code-Switching and Code-Meshing." Her explanation captures some of the nuances and complications of this debate.

> For my visualization, I contrasted code-switching and code-meshing. The upper drawing is a representation of code-switching. The arrow demonstrates a movement between standard English and the undervalued variety of English that the speaker uses as a home language. Although code-switching does allow for the use of both languages, it retains and reaffirms the linguistic hierarchy implicit in American language ideology and continues to place standard English on a pedestal. The two varieties of English might be presented as equal, Vershawn Ashanti Young argued, until they "meet in 'formal settings,' where they are not treated as equals and are not even allowed to mix" (p. 61). In my visualization, I demonstrated this inequality by elevating "standard English" above the "undervalued" variety.
>
> The picture on the lower half of the page represents code-meshing. In contrast to code switching, code-meshing, Young explained, "presents an alternative vision of language to teachers, one that offers the 'disempowered' a more egalitarian path to Standard English, a route that integrates academic English with their own dialects and that simultaneously seeks to end discrimination" (p. 56). I attempted to show this integration by combining the phrases "standard English" and "undervalued variety"—visually meshing the words. Young also refers to the egalitarian nature of code-meshing, the two varieties being treated as equal. In opposition to the drawing above, in which the privileging of standard English is demonstrated by its hierarchical placement on the page, here standard English and the undervalued variety are on the same level. To visualize code-meshing's refusal to privilege one variety over the other, I used a construction level to show that neither variety is elevated over the other.

The objects Ella uses are metaphors rich with possibility, especially when discussing the complex concepts of code-switching and code-meshing. The pedestal is particularly apt in this discussion, in which someone always brings up "standard English." Ella has drawn "standardized English" on the pedestal. Everyone knows that an object is not inherently part of a pedestal but a separate entity. A thing must be put on the pedestal—placed there by a human being. This analogy can help students understand the *ized* in "standardized English," a concept some students seem to have trouble processing. In the same way humans have to place something on a pedestal, humans have to place one version of English above another. The term *standardized English* instead of *standard English*, as mentioned elsewhere, is meant to remind readers that the concept of a prestige language is a constructed one. People make a language "standard." They standardize it. It is humans who place a language on a pedestal, as it were. This is an important point that Ella's simple but brilliant pedestal sketch could be used to illuminate.

Another aspect of Ella's project that could help enrich the learning of other students is her use of a critical quotation from Young et al. She seamlessly weaves together her summary of the book we had been reading that semester with representative phrases from it. Not only does this snippet remind students of Young's argument, it models for them how to use quotations effectively in an analysis. In addition to the discussion, debate, and review that happen when students show their sketches and explain them to the class, individual students must review at least one critical idea from the readings so far. Some, like Ella, incorporate key arguments from scholars, including direct quotations and page numbers. When an excellent thinker and writer like Ella shows her sketch to the class and explains it, that may help other students better understand these complex ideas. Her explanation also can model for less experienced students how to incorporate key ideas from scholars by using partial quotations.

When I responded to Ella about her work, I praised both the simplicity of her juxtaposed images as well as their potential as a point of departure for deeper discussions. Her metaphor involving the construction level is steeped in possibilities for continuing the analogy. It must be noted that it's entirely possible that not everyone in the class knew what that tool was or had ever seen one. Ella and I explained it briefly. For example, the bubbles in the level, which indicate whether something is on a level plane, must have certain conditions met before they become centered in the little glass gauges of the level. If things are uneven, the level, or more likely the thing being tested, must be moved or tweaked so that the bubbles can adjust, can seat themselves on a plane that is level so that they are in the middle of their spaces. The floor, or picture frame, must already be level, or made level, or the bubbles will scoot to one side or the other of their windows. Similarly, if code-meshing is to work in stopping one variety of language routinely being placed above another, the culture has to be amenable to that. If society is not already level, or made level, if the world is not ready for code-meshing, its power as a communicative and rhetorical tool might be limited. On the other hand, it's possible that wide use of code-meshing, even in a still-hierarchical culture, might act as an enzyme to stimulate that leveling of power. Ella's sketch can help us see these implications fairly quickly. Studying her juxtaposed visual representation, viewers are literally all on the same page.

Code-Switching Versus Code-Meshing

Another student who grapples with language controversies is Shauna, who uses both metaphor and color to make her visual argument regarding code-switching versus code-meshing, as shown in Figure 2.7.

Here is how Shauna describes her visual project, called "(Code) Switching vs. Meshing":

> After reading *Other People's English*, I became fascinated with the distinction between code-switching and code-meshing (among educators, not linguists) and all of the racial, social, and pedagogical implications of such a distinction. My visual representation is an attempt to show some of the implications, according to Young et al.

Figure 2.7. Shauna's JVR Depicting Code-Switching Versus Code-Meshing

Two juxtaposed sketches. The left side, labeled "Code-Switching," has a red circle on the top of the page, separated by two rows of barbed wire from a blue circle on the bottom. The red circle has eight little white squares inside it. The blue circle has over twenty little black triangles inside it. The top scene has two green deciduous trees, while the bottom scene has a two palm trees. At the border is a lookout tower, spotlight, and guard tower. One of the black triangles is on a road but stopped at the barbed wire. This triangle has a question mark in a thought bubble. On the right, the red circle and the blue circle are now merged a bit and sit on an equal plane, not one above and one below. They are drawn not in solid lines, like on the left side, but in dotted lines. The intersected section, where the red and blue and red circles intersect, is now purple, and it is peopled by a number of both squares and triangles, which have blended their white and black colors to form grey. In this scene on the right side of the page are comforting things: a recliner, a throw rug, a plant, a lit lamp, and a dog.

On the left side, I have two distinct circles filled with different colors and shapes. The white squares, drawn at the top of the page, reflect the dominant discourse, while the black triangles reflect any number of undervalued dialects. (Note: I deliberately colored the triangles black to reiterate the racial undertones and segregation that result from code-switching. There are also more triangles to imply there are more speakers of "non-standard" languages.) They are separated by "gatekeepers"—a barbed-wire fence, lookout tower, and guard hut—into two geographical locations (indicated by different trees, one species more "exotic" than the other). When a triangle from the lower half attempts to cross the border into the upper half to be with the squares, it is stopped and asked for identification. This leads to confusion (the question mark) for the triangle. Code-switching reinforces the belief that certain varieties or dialects should remain in their respective "appropriate" places, but my visual encourages the viewer to consider the linguistic—and personal identify—confusion that might result from such segregation. Why must a speaker identify her dialect only to then be forced to leave it behind?

The right side of the drawing, my interpretation of code-meshing, has no hierarchy. Instead of the squares being higher than the triangles and protected by guards and barbed wire, the circles are connected on the same horizontal plane to show overlap, creating purple from the previously separate blue and red. The white of the squares and the black of the triangles also combine to create a shade of grey in the middle of the overlapping circles. Because code-meshing mixes varieties or dialects, linguistic integration occurs. Speakers are able to use either or both/all of their dialects depending on the meaning they want to convey (I deliberately created dotted lines in the middle and on the edges of the circles). This process, according to Young et al., is more natural, which is why I chose to draw comfortable homey surroundings, including a bed and a recliner. When a speaker can use both/all of her dialects instead of segregating them into separate places and identities, she is more relaxed and therefore more expressive.

As I wrote to Shauna a few days later, this drawing and explanation provide an excellent point of departure for discussion of the complex controversies surrounding code-switching, code-meshing, race, and Standard English. She draws a provocative analogy between the separation of languages and the literal separation (via the barbed wire) of some groups that wish to come to the United States or to become successful here. Some of the details in her drawing on the left side—the barbed wire, lookout tower, spotlight, and guard hut—suggestive of a prison setting, are also powerful. It occurred to me later that these language issues are not unrelated to the school-to-prison pipeline issues that ruin the lives of so many young people of color today. Some details on the code-meshing side also escaped me until later: the blended, now universally grey (instead of black and white) squares and triangles, no longer positioned in a hierarchy, are also a significant part of the code-meshing debate. Warranting further discussion is how code-switching, although perhaps well-intentioned, can reinscribe language hierarchies. Code-meshing has the potential to interrogate and explode those hierarchies, much like Shauna's circles now intersect and sit on the same horizontal plane. Shauna's question in her written explanation is also worthy of more attention: "Why must a speaker identify her dialect only to then be forced to leave it behind?"

The future English and writing teachers/instructors I teach have a strong sense of social justice. They want to do right by all their students, and many of them are intrigued by the possibilities code-meshing may offer to treat everybody's home language with respect. They're also excited about the possibilities code-meshing offers to enrich writing used both outside and inside academia. At the same time, their JVRs and their explanations of them offer rich opportunities to explore the racist attitudes and assumptions built into traditional English curricula regarding standard English, the groups who speak it, and the groups who don't. When I teach about this language issue in the future, I will add to this mix a term Baker-Bell (2020, citing Paris, 2012) uses, "White Mainstream English" in her discussion of what she calls "Black Language" and how students who speak Black Language are treated (p. 29). Discussing the JVRs on this topic that these preservice teachers sketched, as well as the different terms people use to describe language variations, can help us to imagine the effects certain language policies and practices have on real students whose home language is not exactly like overprivileged academic dialects.

The metaphors and analogies many students displayed in their JVRs could help all of us to better imagine the stakes involved in these and other current debates in English education: teachers' responses to student writing, how new learners of English are treated, the use of students' devices in class, the accessibility of course materials for students with disabilities, the teacher's stance on what gets called "standard English," and so on. The metaphors, drama, and pathos included in JVRs provided many opportunities to review and explore further the discussions that followed our course readings. They helped us to understand more deeply the implications of our practices. In retrospect, I would have added even more class time to discuss further the insights tucked into students' juxtaposed visual representations.

CHAPTER 3

Sketches as Formative Assessment

Students' juxtaposed visual representations also can function as formative assessment, providing a quick way to see what these preservice teachers are getting from the course. To what extent are students just parroting back textbook definitions of important words and phrases—concepts critical to course content—and to what extent do they really understand not just the definitions, but the implications or applications of those ideas? These sketches, because they contrast and illustrate concepts, are a quick way to assess conceptual understanding. They show when students are grasping important differences between ideas or approaches, and when they might be misunderstanding crucial differences. The drawings themselves, or sometimes the writing and discussing that follow the sketching session, also can lead us all to deeper insights about concepts or controversies—points we didn't think of after reading articles or chapters about them. In other cases, when a student illustrates concepts that we have not discussed in class, it can reveal a misunderstanding, yes, but it also can reveal connections they are making that had not occurred to me. JVRs that are "wrong" in one sense provide an opportunity to explore related issues that are important to the student who drew the representation.

Since the main purpose of having students do these JVRs is to stimulate discussion and understanding, in some ways this chapter on formative assessment is an anomaly, because I do not assign JVRs primarily to assess students. As I discovered, however, sometimes students' sketches and accompanying written explanations revealed that they did not completely understand a concept we had studied. I do not penalize students for what their sketches reveal, but I use the sketches as an opportunity to revisit the concepts, teach them again, and check up on students' understanding later through an exam question or discussion topic.

As explained in Chapter 1, before I ask students to visually represent concepts, I show them one or two of mine, usually sketching on the board a couple of concepts we currently are discussing. As I'm planning a class session, for example, I try to think of which concepts we're studying that week that might be particularly challenging for future writing instructors but important for them to understand: for example, *situated ethos* versus *invented ethos*.

Sometimes I'll show them a previous sketch I've done, mostly to ease their minds about the technical quality of the drawings I'm expecting. I don't show them lots of JVR examples, however, because I'm afraid it might truncate their own conceptualization of those concepts. But once we've all drawn something, I may start by showing them mine just to get the ball rolling and to demonstrate to them that using stick figures or kindergarten-level renderings is fine. It's the attempt to represent that matters more than the representation itself.

I typically ask my students to do two or three quick sketches in class over the course of the semester, incorporating them into a class session only occasionally, and only when we're discussing concepts or ideas I think might require more discussion and clarification. These in-class sketches are never graded, and students can choose whether they wish to show them and explain them to us via the projector. I also assign a low-stakes visual reading response (5% of grade) due late in the semester. I assess this latter project generously because I mainly want students to have another opportunity to produce a JVR, and I want them to be able to take their time.

However, as we examined and discussed some of these sketches in class, or as I analyzed them more closely for this project, I sometimes have been surprised by what they revealed. As simple as some of the sketches are, they can show who understands—or does not—a fundamental concept from the class, one I was sure had been made perfectly clear. Happily, sometimes another student's sketch helps clarify a complex concept that may have been misrepresented in a previous sketch. More often than I would have predicted, however, the formative assessment they provide is a well-placed check on my rosy assumptions, prompting further review, explanation, or clarifying discussion. Like other useful formative assessment tools, they show me the gaps in my pedagogy.

In this chapter, I discuss a selection of JVRs that were epiphanies for me, helping me realize that my teaching had failed some students regarding key concepts in literacy and the teaching of writing, and I suggest ways other teacher educators might use JVRs as quick but necessary checks on what their students are learning. Foregrounding these sketches should not be seen as a negative reflection on individual students, but rather as a reflection on something missing in my teaching. These sketches taught me where I needed to adjust my pedagogy in order to better teach what some state standards call "content-specific words and phrases." Sometimes these terms represent complex material, especially material that is counterintuitive or involves concepts that challenge commonly accepted assumptions about writing, language, and assessment. Each teacher educator must determine what concepts in their course are critical in order for students to reach a higher level in their learning and knowledge. Meyer and Land (2003) refer to such ideas as "threshold concepts," which involve understanding a crucial disciplinary idea that goes way beyond simple factual material. Often this deeper understanding requires a shift in perception or point of view, or even a contradiction of previous unspoken assumptions. Perkins (1999) calls this "troublesome knowledge," and it can require different interventions. Mastering threshold concepts and troublesome knowledge allows learners to move forward in a particular discipline. Contrasted sketches can help teachers assess whether students have mastered that challenging material.

TEACHING TROUBLESOME KNOWLEDGE

The sketches in this chapter show how I was able to use student sketches to informally assess students' conceptual understanding of complex ideas. Seeing what concepts some students contrasted and what they said about those concepts showed me what I needed to reteach regarding ideas essential to the teaching of writing, the purpose of my class. For my students, future teachers of English language arts (ELA), literacy, and writing, some widely accepted but misguided ideas about writing and English need to be interrogated in order for their students to develop motivation and agency regarding their writing. Those qualities are essential to students fulfilling, for example, the challenging writing requirements present in most state standards. Although my future teachers needed to learn many ideas and practices in order to support their students' writing development, in this chapter I examine just a few ideas that seemed to give students more trouble than others.

One concept that some students had trouble with—and it is an important one for new teachers to grasp if they are to respect the different languages and dialects of English that their students bring with them to school—is "standardized English." This term has profound implications regarding issues of diversity and inclusion because the assumptions underpinning "standard" can affect the way teachers respond to their students' speech and writing.

In my classes for preservice teachers on the teaching of writing and in my linguistics class, understanding why we might employ *standardized* English as a replacement for *standard* English is critical in order for these future teachers (and their students) to see the racial injustice that plays out through oppressive language practices in our culture. Both terms describe the formal language purportedly "appropriate" for use in school, business, and much professional communication. However, as many scholars in literacy today have argued (Baker-Bell, 2020; Clark & Ivanic, 1997; Gilyard, 2000; Lippi-Green, 2012; Young et al., 2014), the emphasis on *standard* English is fraught with issues regarding race, class, and gender that can impede students' development as writers. The term *standardized English* is preferred by many today because the *ized* suffix means that language is *made* "standard." The *ized* draws attention to the human role in declaring one dialect preferred over another. The use of "standard*ized*" invites an exploration of the privileged class's vested interest in choosing a dialect used by themselves as the "standard" one, when, as most linguists argue, all dialects are equally sophisticated. As Keith Gilyard, former National Council of Teachers of English president and former Conference on College Composition and Communication chair, said in his 2000 Chair's Address to that organization, "The standardized variety was selected by the linguistic elite" (p. 267). The word *standard* English makes it seem as though this variety of English is inherently better than any other, with no human manipulation in the process. The word *standardized*, on the other hand, reflects the more accurate idea that this form of English has been deemed as such by the very people whose home language is most like this version of English. In their explanation of these terms, Lindblom and Christenbury (2018, p. 143) cite Gilyard (2000), who spoke of the difference between these terms in *College Composition and Communication*: "Get that IZE up there and you can focus more on the fact that the standardIZED variety was selected by the linguistic elite" (p. 267). This difference is critical for teachers to understand, not just for the meaning of the added suffix *ized*, but for the implications this difference should make for teaching.

How might those four letters affect teaching? There's a good chance that a writing instructor who believes that standard English is a fixed, neutral, and superior version of the language will treat students' writing and speaking very differently than a teacher who understands that a certain dialect of English has been declared the preferred one by people who happen to speak that dialect. The teacher who understands, as do most linguists, that all languages are rule-bound and systematic may be more likely to see language as fluid, always evolving, and put into categories of worth by people in power who have a vested interest in declaring some versions of English "standard" and some "nonstandard." This understanding will have implications regarding the extent to which teachers respect their students' versions of English, how they react to their students' speech, and how they respond to their students' writing—all of which affect how much their students can learn in those teachers' classes.

In many of my classes, the difference between "standard" and "standardized" is part of the troublesome knowledge Perkins (1999) identified, knowledge that may contradict some deep assumptions students hold about language. The difference between these two words is also a threshold concept (Meyer & Land, 2003) of the kind described earlier, one that students must master in order to move forward in their discipline. Progress and insight in teaching writing are dependent on knowing those two terms and their implications. A deep understanding of why some scholars replace "standard" with "standardized" can help students teach for social justice. It also can give students an impetus to experiment with language, developing their language and style to reach the readers they want to reach and, in the words of a NYSED Next Generation Standard, to understand "that usage is a matter of convention that can change over time" and that there are various ways to "resolve issues of complex or contested usage" (NYSED, Conventions of Academic English/Language for Learning, Grades 9–12 Anchor Standard L1, 2017, Appendix A, p. 123).

What I wanted this class of future teachers to understand is that so-called "standard" English arbitrarily has been declared to be so by those in power and with a vested interest in making their dialect of English the formal, accepted one for school and for high-stakes assessments. Students can develop, to some extent, this sophisticated view of language by understanding that language shifts and changes because of time, context, and human influence, not because of an infallible decree from one usage book written in stone. The word *standardized* can promote this more linguistically informed view of language and may help struggling writers become less intimidated by what can seem like rigid, arbitrary rules connected with writing.

In the next section, I discuss how seeing what students were *not* getting regarding these concepts helped me rethink my pedagogy: what articles I might switch out or add next semester, what focused discussions I might include to address difficult material, and how I might find out earlier in the semester where understanding started to go off the rails for some students.

ASSESSING CONCEPTUAL UNDERSTANDING

I wanted these preservice teachers to literally see that the *ized* in standardized English is meant to emphasize the constructedness of language preference and the power it gives to groups in charge of that construction. This is an issue directly related to teachers' views of diversity and the decisions they make in their teaching of writing. Once I finished my quickly scribbled representation, I projected it first and explained it, partly to model the process of oral explanation, but mostly to break the ice, to demonstrate that if the professor can show a very rough sketch to the class and explain it, students can, too. They need not be ashamed of what may be very simple drawings. To illustrate the difference between standard English and standardized English, and to put students' minds at ease regarding sketching talent, I drew the rendering shown in Figure 3.1, using a wall as a metaphor.

What I like about my sketch is that the stick figures on the "Standardized English" side are actively building their walls, constructing them, while the wall on the left appears complete and static. On the right, the builders' hands are on the large bricks, and one figure is bending over to pick one up. This shows human involvement in the making of the "wall" that acts as a barrier for so many people. In different areas of the sketch, there are different walls being built, with different-sized and -shaped bricks. This was

Figure 3.1. Dunn's JVR of Standard English Versus Standardized English

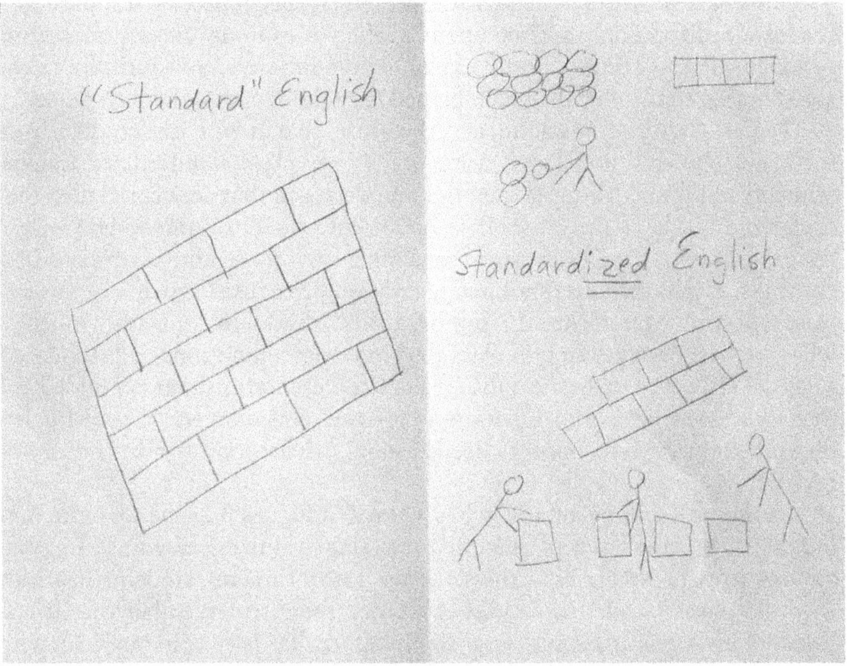

Two juxtaposed sketches. On the left side, under "Standard English," is a brick wall that looks finished. No human beings are in sight, intimating that the wall simply exists on its own and was always there. Juxtaposed on the right, as "Standard*ized* English," are several unfinished walls in different areas being built by stick figures. Each wall under construction differs from the others by the size and shape of the bricks being used to build it. The sketch on the right, the "Standard*ized* English" side, shows that it is people that construct walls, like people construct what is considered "standard."

an attempt to show that even standardized English is not so standard after all. People may refer to standard English or demand it of their employees or students, but linguists know (as should preservice literacy teachers) that standard English shifts and changes continually, and what some judges-of-others'-language consider to be the ideal norm, others may consider passé or offensive. (For further discussion of these differences, see Bryan Garner's *Modern English Usage*, 2009.)

This representation pops into my mind whenever I'm thinking about "standard" and "standardized." It helps cement for me the theoretical concept of constructedness. It also demonstrates the power of the picture-superiority effect (Childers & Houston, 1984), based on studies showing that people remember information associated with images more vividly and for a longer period of time than they do information presented without images. A student who was in the class in which I showed my wall sketch was also in a subsequent class with me. When the subject of standard versus standardized English came up, as it often does in my classes on writing or language, this student orally explained the differences beautifully to the class, noting that my wall sketch helped them understand the difference.

I can say with some confidence, therefore, that at least one student from the class who saw my sketch using walls to explain standardized English remembered it and said it helped them understand that concept. Sadly, that sketch did not have the same effect on another student, Emma, who was in the same class. I have to assume that Emma saw my rendition of the different walls. Her sketch disappointed me not only because I saw it as a misrepresentation of "standardized," but because it seemed to contradict much of what we had been reading in class that interrogated notions of "standard" English. However, it was Emma's visual representation that reminded me that these sketches could function as formative assessment, a tool for letting me know which concepts needed more instruction, demonstration, or review.

In Emma's side-by-side sketches, shown in Figure 3.2, she was attempting to contrast the concept of *standard* as opposed to *standardized* English, an idea stressed throughout the semester. Every time my students heard or used the phrase *standard English*, I wanted them to remember that it is a category invented by people. English, therefore, has been standard*ized*, with the *ized* in that word doing the same job as the *ized* in hypnot*ized*, homogen*ized*, or priorit*ized*, that is, not something that just exists on its own, but has been made that way by human beings. In Emma's sketch, however, we see that she had a very different idea of what *standardized* means, using it as a name for students' home or heritage language.

Here is Emma's written description of this visual representation, which she calls "Standard Versus Standardized":

> This visual representation juxtaposes standard and standardized English. The first box shows a girl trying to read directions to create a bookcase. The steps are formal and use standard English. This form of English is grammatically correct and has vocabulary that is the social norm of the country. The girl has trouble trying to understand the formal structure as it is not specially targeting her and does not have the dialect she is comfortable with. The vocabulary seen in the directions confuses her and she cannot put the bookcase together. In box two, the girl has directions that are specifically for New York and has photos alongside words she is accustomed to seeing. Here, she is able to understand the steps and put together the furniture. Overall, this visual representation targets the underlying issue of standard English. This dominating form of English has many young speakers see it as an oppressor form of writing, as they are more accustomed

Figure 3.2. Emma's JVR on "Standard" Versus "Standardized" English

Two juxtaposed sketches. On the left side, labeled "Standard," a woman holds a list labeled "Steps U.S.," which are directions for assembling an IKEA product that sits in a box nearby. She has a sad face. The product remains unassembled. On the right, labeled "Standardized," the same woman is smiling. She is holding directions called "Steps NY," which has illustrations on it. Next to her is a fully assembled bookcase.

to the standardized way that highlights their cultural identity, history, and pride. This boundary between understanding one another is important to approach in a writing class and it is important to explain standard English to students so they can connect to communicate to others who do not use standardized English alongside them.

There are parts of Emma's explanation that have elements of what I wanted students to understand. She does see "formal," standard English as the "dominating form" that many young people see as "an oppressor form of writing." She also understands that the language students use in their own communities (in this case, what she calls "New York") can be a more "comfortable" form for them.

However, her sketches and her explanation ultimately display the *opposite* of the concept I was trying to teach. It's not the dominant, "grammatically correct," "formal," and "oppressor form" of English that she characterizes as *standardized*. Instead, she calls the *students'* language *standardized*, the language that "highlights their cultural identity, history, and pride." While I'm pleased that she sees the value in students' heritage language, I wish she had examined further the human agency responsible for making formal English the "oppressor form." She never delves into the very human manipulation of standard English, which also reflects the cultural identity and history of the privileged class who have the power to declare what is the "standard" version of English, which happens to be the version used by that same privileged class.

At the end of her explanation, Emma stated: "It is important to explain standard English to students so they can connect to communicate to others who do not use standardized English alongside them." She's right, of course, that writers need to consider their readers. And she's not wrong that a student's home language is also standardized over time by the community that uses that language. But her implication that students must blithely conform to the dialect of the privileged class is precisely the common belief that I was trying to get these future English teachers to interrogate. I wanted them to question standard English, to understand how it came to be "standard," and the possible deleterious effect this imposed, rigid view of correctness can have on the very students Emma seems sympathetic to. Granted, students should be taught to communicate to a variety of readers, but here she seems to be putting standard English right back in the same entitled position it has always been in, without questioning the vested human role in putting it there. She's applying the word *standardized* to the language "New York" students speak, instead of using that word to disrupt societal assumptions that standard English is inherently better than other Englishes. I'm glad Emma made this sketch, wrote her explanation of it, and was generous enough to share it with us. It made me realize that I needed to do much more to help students see past embedded beliefs that oppressive language practices should just continue as usual.

Emma's sketch and written description, a kind of *transmediation* (the act of translating or transforming ideas from one medium to another), showed me something about her grasp of this concept that I hadn't seen before. Hadjioannou and Hutchinson (2014) summarize a number of studies that demonstrate the power of transmediation to uncover cultural assumptions. In their article that appeared in the *International Journal of Multicultural Education*, they argue that transmediation "appears particularly promising in supporting multicultural education through fostering critical awareness of values and biases underpinning conventions" (p. 2). Citing Shor (1999) and Semali (2002), they promote multimodal interpretations as "fertile grounds for questioning social norms [and] power relations," and "a tool that invites critical considerations that can support conversations about class, race, and gender" (p. 3). Emma's sketch did exactly that. It showed me how deeply embedded beliefs are held.

If preservice teachers have a concretized belief in the inherent good-
ness or inevitability of standard English, correctness, and "vocabulary
that is the social norm of the country," introducing them to *standardized
English*, a mere term that's meant to question that ingrained belief, cannot
by itself change this perceived dogma. This sketch taught me that I need
to do more to help them unlearn some societal "givens" before they can
fully grasp the constructedness of language preferences. Widely accepted
beliefs, called commonplaces, keep their power by being invisible. These
deeply held assumptions may be why preservice teachers learn, or partly
learn, one thing about language in their literacy methods classes but revert
to previous beliefs about language when they teach their own classes. The
threshold concept that society's judgments about language are constructed
may be particularly difficult for students to fully understand, let alone
apply.

Emma did this visual representation for the late-semester graded project. It was not simply sketched out in 10 minutes of class time. What's more,
she produced it after we had read a lot about the challenges to "standard"
English, articles on code-meshing, on translanguaging, and so on, all of
which questioned to some extent conventional views of "correct" English
(Guerra, 2012; Smitherman, 2012; Young et al., 2014). We had discussed
such readings at length. She also produced this after what I thought of as
my insightful sketch about standard versus standardized English through
the visual metaphor of humans building different walls. So I must admit that
my visual representation did not help her change her concept of "standard."
Thus, her visual representation became not only a snapshot of what Emma
was thinking, but an assessment of my teaching.

Since these sketches were discussed very late in the semester, my interventions for teaching this concept more thoroughly would have to be applied
the next semester. In the future, there are a number of changes I can make in
my pedagogy. First, I might add Gilyard's (2000) keynote address to the syllabus, or perhaps find a video clip of the most relevant parts online, where
he talks about the importance of literacy teachers getting students to think
critically about language hierarchies. I also might add to the class readings
a snippet of the Clark and Ivanic (1997) text that Gilyard credits for the
"standard/standardized" argument. I might explore additional linguistics
texts (such as April Baker-Bell's *Linguistic Justice*, 2020), or videos that
explain and demonstrate in an engaging way how some dialects come to
be the preferred ones. After reading and discussing relevant works, I could
spot-check understanding by having students fill in quick sentence starters
like these on index cards or online surveys:

- The difference between standard and standardized English is
  that_____

- Gilyard argues that we should add *ized* to "standard" English because doing so would _____
- The use of "standard" English, without the *ized* at the end, makes it seem that _____. However, the use of "standardized" English draws attention to _____

Students also might discuss their answers in small groups or breakout rooms as a check on themselves, then share aloud with us their group's collaboratively agreed-upon response to those sentence starters.

This difficulty I now see that some students have in rethinking their previous assumptions about *standard*—how it's not born standard but made that way, and how it's not even standard over time and place—sent me back to the drawing board, so to speak. I saw that troublesome knowledge was a bigger barrier than I had realized. These revelatory sketches invite me to brainstorm some other dramatic ways to get students to see why developing a deeper understanding of the complex but critical difference between these two words should affect the way they teach writing. What will help them analyze the hypothetical difference, for example, between a teacher who blithely uses the term *standard* English and another who uses the term *standardized*, knowing full well the significance of that suffix?

How can I demonstrate that standard English is not entirely standard across the world? One way might be to look at the same day's news in *The New York Times*, and *The Times of India*, *The Guardian*, *China Daily*, or *The Sydney Morning Herald*. Would the "standard" be the same, or would each news outlet be adhering to its own in-house style guide? What would demonstrate how language changes over time? Maybe we could examine front-page newspaper articles from 150 or 100 or even 30 years ago and compare them with the same newspaper's front pages now. How might the vocabulary or sentence structure or usage have changed over the decades? If those analyses proved too complicated or time-consuming, I simply might have students read *Garner's Modern English Usage* entries on "irregardless," "disinterested," or "literally" to see how rants about those words have intensified over time, only to eventually have them added to respectable dictionaries. Or I just might have students google "Oxford comma" and see how online fights still erupt today between people who simply are using a different usage manual. (My co-written book with Ken Lindblom, *Grammar Rants: How a Backstage Tour of Writing Complaints Can Help Students Make Informed, Savvy Choices About Their Writing* [2011], has many examples of vicious but silly fights about "grammar" that can be found easily on the Internet.)

Another lesson I learned from the contrasted sketch in this section is that I would have students do these quick sketches much earlier in the semester, shortly after we read and discussed these concepts, or perhaps a few weeks later as a review. Then, if some students still struggled with these different terms, there would be time left to try something else. Because these two words represent concepts far more complex than their single-word appearance might suggest, and also because *standardized* might challenge deeply held but perhaps subconscious assumptions about language, students sometimes need time to digest the meaning of *standardized* and see how its implications play out in society.

PROMOTING DEEPER LEARNING

Other JVRs functioned for me not so much as a summative assessment of individual students but as a "reading-of-the-room" tool, especially as my previous assumptions had not been quite accurate regarding some students' understanding of language change and power dynamics. Another JVR that resulted from a 10-minute, in-class sketching session (from a class for preservice teachers on the teaching of writing) also revealed to me that a student either did not understand what I was trying to teach about what teachers should prioritize when responding to writing, or was not convinced by the research and scholarship we'd been reading. The issue concerned whether, when, and how much to focus on a writer's ideas or errors. Briefly, researchers and scholars in the field of rhetoric and composition universally recommend, based on decades of research, that instructors responding to students' drafts should address content and idea development first, saving the focus on surface errors for later in the process. To insist that students fix spelling and grammatical errors first, before they have fully developed their ideas, can make writers disinclined to add more text or, say, delete an irrelevant paragraph that they had just spent much time proofreading carefully. I teach these future writing instructors that editing is, of course, critical, but that students' ideas should be commented upon first. In the sketch in Figure 3.3, Sacha juxtaposes a writing environment that emphasizes content and one that emphasizes "spelling/grammar."

Here is how Sacha describes the sketch: "In class, if we focus too much on content and not enough on spelling/grammar, students will never learn." Sacha's sketch and explanation dismayed me. I saw them as both a misinterpretation and rejection of practices I had been advocating, and the scholars we had been reading had been advocating (Anson, 2000; Anson & Anson, 2017; Calhoon-Dillahunt & Forrest, 2013; Daiker, 1989; Mack, 2013). Since the beginning of the semester, we had been discussing the importance of responding to students' ideas, especially in early drafts, before slamming students for every minor surface error. We also had been talking about how to help students see how writing, especially authentic (real-world) writing, could empower them—beyond the goal of scoring high on a standardized test. This attention to content, and handling of error later, once a draft has materialized a bit, is a fairly well-known and accepted practice

Figure 3.3. Sacha's JVR on Teachers' Attention to Error

Two scenes juxtaposed. On the left side of the page, labeled "In Class," a teacher gives a writing assignment: "Write about what you did yesterday." A student's paper, which has received an "A+," says: "We went to the store and their was a cat on the street." On the left side, labeled "On Test," there is the same prompt, and the student has written the same sentence, but with both "there" and "street" spelled wrong and circled in red. The test paper has received a "C."

in composition/rhetoric and writing studies, as is the view that a teacher's relentless attention to every error, without engaging with the writer's ideas, can be harmful to young writers, especially those whose writing has long been picked apart in previous grades.

In my classes these ideas were never presented as an either/or situation. I never said that teachers could not ever point out errors or assess students using careful proofreading as a criterion. In fact, we had read articles on style and sentence combining, how to help students vary the length and structure of their sentences, and also how to transition smoothly from one idea to the next. We had discussed much more than "content." We also practiced how to locate and prioritize *patterns* of error to focus on, patterns most likely to interfere with meaning: to triage perceived problems in a student's paper, not ignore them. Finally, we also discussed when was the best time to focus on editing, that it was far more practical to do close proofreading not on an early draft, but when a piece of writing was nearing completion. Not one article did we read that said or implied that students should receive A+ grades on unedited work. Nor did I.

Therefore, I initially was disappointed with Sacha's reductive representation of this process. However, her sketch was a formative assessment tool, helping me gauge to what extent this one student (and likely others) understood and/or accepted the recommendation that teachers strategize their response to error, considering the stage of the draft (first or final), the development of ideas, and the pattern and priority of the errors found. Her sketch also showed me to what extent my pedagogy had succeeded (or not) in helping all my students understand the response and revising practices I had been teaching. It taught me what I should have already known and what researcher Donald Daiker (1989) had argued 30 years ago: that teachers correcting errors, and correcting them relentlessly, is an almost ingrained ritual, an iron-clad commonplace, one not easily changed. And "corrections" are often stylistic preferences. In our previous class discussions on this issue, Sacha never said anything about the way she obviously felt about this issue. The quickly drawn contrasted sketches, however, brought out her real opinion. I'm glad they did.

At the time, we did not discuss Sacha's sketch in detail partly because I did not want to embarrass her by contradicting her, and also because I had not allotted much class time to discuss each student's work. This sketch resulted from a quick in-class exercise. It was used mostly to give students an idea of what visual representation was, since they had a graded project— although a low-stakes one—on visual representation near the end of the semester. In that short span of class time, I simply wanted to give them a chance to practice, to model the process for them, and to lightly sample the class in terms of what concepts they thought were important and how they would represent those concepts. In retrospect, I wish I had found a gentle way to ask Sacha for more nuance in her view and to make sure the class didn't think I was agreeing with her stark representation. I was not expecting Sacha's view of these issues. But I will from now on. This representation, however, made me realize that I needed to do some adjusting of my teaching in future classes. It reminded me, once again, that sometimes people have to unlearn some assumptions before they will consider new research or better teaching practices.

Visualizing Controversies

Fortunately, however, Brigid's sketch, produced during the same in-class session and shown in Figure 3.4, acted as a counterweight to Sacha's. Brigid, too, juxtaposed the effect on students of direct teaching of grammar, but with a very different slant.

Figure 3.4. Brigid's JVR Contrasting Different Ways to Teach Writing

Two scenes juxtaposed. On the left is a classroom with a stern-looking teacher pointing to a board covered with "Grammar Rules." At the end of the list of rules it says, "Now Write!" A student with a sad face sits at a desk with a pencil in hand. A big question mark is on their paper, and question marks surround their head. On the right is another classroom with a smiling teacher standing next to a board that says, "Get your ideas down! Start writing!" A student with a happy face and a lightbulb over their head is writing words on a sheet of paper on their desk.

Here is what Brigid wrote about her sketch:

> If you focus very heavily on grammar, students may get overwhelmed and confused, and feel as though they can't write and follow all the rules. If you let student writers then go back and revisit consistent grammatical mistakes after they've started the writing process, they may learn grammar in a more contextual way, and also not get overwhelmed from a heavy grammar lesson.

It might be argued that Brigid's sketch, also produced in about 10 minutes of class time, reduces some complex ideas into something that seems too easy. Not all students happily scribble away simply by having a teacher tell them to get their ideas down. But the point of these visual representations is to get the gist of what students are thinking or to open conversations. In retrospect, it might have been interesting to take one photo juxtaposing the two JVRs and project them on the same screen: two different views of a content/grammar emphasis fight, which we could then discuss together and which would add some nuance to the debate. We would need more time than I had scheduled for this exercise to discuss the sketches together in this way, and I'd have to find a way to do so without embarrassing the students who generously had volunteered to have their sketches shown to the class. But in the future, I will need to build in more time to examine these issues, which I previously had not thought were controversial. I also may want to preview the sketches before I show them and design the order of presentation for the best pedagogical effect.

Revealing Misunderstandings

Another sketch produced a revelation I did not expect. In this instance, I learned that one student, Maura, either didn't understand, or didn't agree with, ideas about authentic (real-world) writing instruction that we had been reading about and that I had been trying to convince students to adopt. Her sketch was off-topic, that is, not representative of course content. This realization does not reflect negatively on her, and her sketch illustrated some creative ideas, but it made me reflect on how I'll need to approach this topic in future classes and what different interventions I might use for cases like this one.

First, some background. No amount of teaching will result in students learning to write better if the students themselves are not invested in writing, revising, and proofreading. It takes time, focus, and at least a bit of genuine engagement to produce decent writing. Not everyone is motivated by school writing aimed at the teacher just to obtain a grade. This is why many researchers and scholars promote "authentic writing," that is, writing in a variety of genres, for different purposes, and aimed at a variety of readers in the world outside school (Hallman, 2009; Lindblom, 2015; Wiggans, 2009). Of course, some writing and some school genres must be practiced in class, and not all writing aimed at outside readers actually needs to be sent to them. But many more writing projects in school can be designed as if they have a real audience and purpose beyond assessment. (There is an extensive, peer-reviewed blog, founded in 2013 by English educators with expertise in the teaching of writing, that is dedicated to educating the public about pedagogies related to authentic writing: *Teachers, Profs, Parents: Writers Who Care*: https://writerswhocare.wordpress.com.) Teachers can collect dozens of pages from each student, but students' writing and editing may not improve unless and until students see how writing can empower them, enabling them to communicate with readers they care about.

In the sketch in Figure 3.5, we see that Maura does understand the value of engaging writing projects, but she completely ignores authentic writing, a topic we had explored in depth all semester. Maura juxtaposed a sketch

Figure 3.5. Maura's JVR of "Creative Writing Assignments" Versus "The Standard Essay"

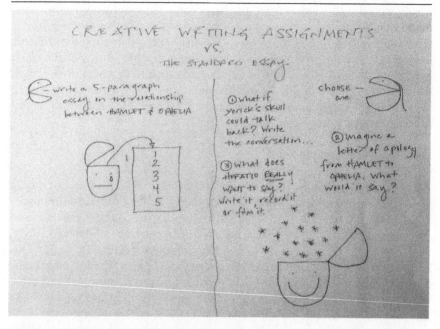

Two juxtaposed images: "Creative Writing Assignments" versus "The Standard Essay." On the left, a teacher's face is saying, "Write a 5-paragraph essay on the relationship between Hamlet and Ophelia." A student's face, with a tear running down, is at the side of a box with the numbers 1–5 going down the page. On the right side of the page, the teacher is saying, "Choose one." There are three choices, and a student's smiling head is opened up, with stars coming out. The choices: (1) What if Yorick's skull could talk back? Write a conversation . . . , (2) Imagine a letter of apology from Hamlet to Ophelia. What would it say? (3) What does Horatio *really* want to say? Write it, record it or film it.

of a sad student who was required to write a five-paragraph theme, to that of a happy student who had some creative choices regarding an essay on *Hamlet*. Yes, she was addressing a writer's motivation. However, our focus in the class had been on the additional motivation that can result when students have opportunities to write in real genres (movie or book review, directions, instructions, travel narrative, public service announcement, letter to the editor, etc.) for a real purpose (to inform, persuade, entertain, amuse, etc., and not just to be assessed), and to a real person outside school (newspaper editor, congressional representative, school superintendent, parent, younger child, student in another country, etc.), even if the piece actually is not sent or submitted. This authentic writing can tap into students' interests, skills, or experiences. It can demonstrate to young writers that they do have something to say and that writing can not only showcase what they know, but also have an impact on the world, or at least on a targeted reader. In this sketch, Maura shows some creative assignments, but they are not authentic (real-world) projects.

Here is Maura's written explanation of her sketch:

Creative Writing Assignments Versus the Standard Essay

My visual representation is meant to show how flat and dull assignments are when the first rule is that they have to fit a standard form. My drawing is meant to show that with a little creativity, assignments can pull the same breadth of textual analysis from the student in much more interesting and engaging ways. Creative assignments can assess similar levels of understanding but allow for a greater range of expression. While the two sides of my drawing are not completely opposite, their perception could be. The assignment on the left seems more like a test of the students' ability to comply, while the choices on the right are concerned with their level of understanding and allow them some flexibility of response.

Granted, Maura's sketch of different ways to analyze characters in *Hamlet* could be used to discuss how to create more engaging assignments instead of the traditional literary analyses written in school. These are good ideas. She illustrates in a simple but clear way how teachers might spark students' creativity when being asked to analyze characters in *Hamlet*. The three choices show innovative ways to get students engaged in the play and in character analysis.

However, Maura's visual representation suggests that she might not have fully understood the concept of *authentic writing* as we used that term in class—that is, writing in a variety of genres for "the real world" as opposed to writing in school aimed only at the teacher. Because I wanted students to think about how they could include authentic writing in their own classes, we never discussed the literature-based creative writing assignments of the kind she describes. Our class focused heavily on getting students to write in a variety of genres for a variety of audiences, mostly outside their classroom walls. That's what made me think she might be conflating *authentic* writing with *creative* writing projects. Or perhaps she simply didn't think students writing for an outside audience was important. It's also possible she was thinking of "authentic" writing in the way many creative writers do, as writing that has an authentic or realistic voice. However, we had discussed those different uses of the word *authentic* throughout the semester, and in virtually every class meeting we examined examples of real-world genres, their textual features, and their targeted readers. We also read much about authentic projects, discussing ways to implement them with students and writing in some real-world genres ourselves earlier in the semester. We never once talked about creative ways to change standard classroom literary essays centered on Shakespeare, valuable as that might be. Although the students repeatedly brought up literary essays—they were, after all, English majors and English master's students—our readings and class discussions centered on just about every other genre *but* literary analysis: travel narratives aimed at specialized websites, public petitions, specialized blogs, public service announcements, and so on. I was surprised, therefore, to see Maura focus on alternative prompts for projects that would be restricted to the immediate classroom environment of a single literature class, projects read and assessed only by the classroom teacher. Her sketch wasn't "wrong." It showed some imagination, and no doubt students would appreciate the choices it offered. But her sketch suggested to me that the class had not convinced her of the value of authentic writing projects and maybe had not even taught her what they are.

While Maura showed excellent alternatives to run-of-the-mill essays on *Hamlet*, this low-stakes visual reading response, due in the last 2 weeks of the semester, was supposed to reflect an issue that we had read about and discussed in this class. Maura's sketch, useful as it was to discuss creative in-class projects on *Hamlet*, had almost nothing to do with what had been the focus of this graduate class. However, her sketch taught me much about what my class had not succeeded in doing. What intervention might address this gap? Happily, other students' sketches often can aid in that additional learning.

One intervention that presented itself was Shelby's representation, whose serendipitous drawing, shown in Figure 3.6, addressed a similar issue. Shelby, like Maura, also chose to show a five-paragraph essay on one side of her page. However, Shelby juxtaposed that standard assignment to "authentic writing," a movie review.

Here is how Shelby describes her sketch:

> In my visual representation, I depict a scenario where a teacher emphasizes the importance of academic writing and the students' negative consensus to it in one panel. In the other panel, another teacher emphasizes the usefulness of authentic writing and the students' overall appreciation for it. In the left panel (academic writing), I put stormy weather in the background to symbolize the students' dread of the five-paragraph assignment. I include an image of the five-paragraph assignment that has an arrow pointing to it, stating the strict importance of academic writing. Next to it is a frowning face, which characterizes the students' unhappiness. In the right panel (authentic writing), there is sunny weather to indicate a good mood. A movie review and arrow pointing to it that praises authentic writing are also present. There is also a smiling face in the panel that denotes the students' happiness. I decided not to draw the teacher because I wanted the students' reactions to be the main focus.

Figure 3.6. Shelby's JVR Contrasting Academic Writing to Authentic Writing

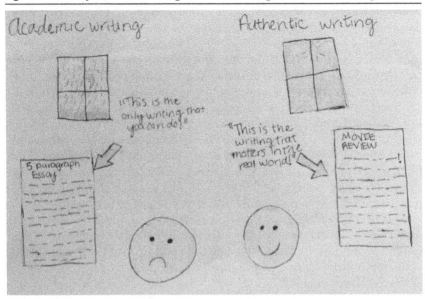

Two scenes juxtaposed: academic writing versus authentic writing. On the left, academic writing is shown. An arrow points at a 5-paragraph essay. A command in quotes says, "This is the only writing that you can do." A window shows there's a storm outside. A student has a sad face. On the right, the authentic writing side, an arrow points to piece of paper labeled "Movie Review." A quote says, "This is the writing that matters in the real world!" A window shows blue skies, sunshine, and green grass. A student has a happy face.

As did Maura, Shelby depicted sadness on the part of students restricted to the five-paragraph essay, and happiness when they were given the opportunity to do something else, but in this case it's the real-world genre of a movie review. Shelby's is a simple sketch, not likely to engender a long discussion, but it told me that she understood the concept of school writing versus authentic writing. Showing Shelby's sketch after Maura's is a good way to revisit these ideas, generate examples, and answer questions. Doing so reinforces the concept of authentic writing as that which is written for a real purpose for an audience beyond the classroom, and it does so without embarrassing Maura.

Opportunities for Interventions

In retrospect, however, Maura's sketch is worth returning to here for the opportunities it offers to consider different interventions, with or without the happy coincidence of Shelby's clarifying sketch depicting authentic writing. Maura's sketch also invites me to reflect on why it frustrated me as much as it did and how I might have taken better advantage of the ideas in her drawings. Unpacking Maura's enthusiasm about the "creative" but classroom-based writing projects on *Hamlet* could address a concern no doubt shared by other preservice teachers, English majors who have spent years reading and analyzing literature, not research and scholarship on writing. We could have discussed elements of her writing projects in relation to authentic writing projects as a way to promote rhetorically savvy writing.

First, even though Maura's assignments are not aimed at the outside world, her invitation for students to take on the point of view of Horatio, or of Yorick's skull, or of a contrite Hamlet, is consistent with perspective shifts required for sophisticated thinking. We could have explored those different perspectives in *Hamlet* and also generated writing ideas regarding perspective shifts in other canonical works. For example, how might imagined perspectives from nonprotagonists in texts open up critical discussions of *To Kill a Mockingbird, Of Mice and Men*, or *The Glass Menagerie*? Such a discussion also would enable us to explore the #DisruptTexts Twitter movement and website (https://disrupttexts.org/) by Tricia Ebarvia, Lorena German, Kimberly N. Parker, and Julia E. Torres, which question racial and other stereotypes in literary texts.

Second, Maura's use of different genres—dialogue, recording, letter, film—no doubt would engage many students, and it arguably does address one of New York State's writing standards, which requires students to write "for a range of tasks, purposes, and audiences" (NYS CCR.W 10). It's an audience of one—the teacher—but the tasks, genres, and hypothetical purposes are varied. What's more, even though students must write about *Hamlet*, Maura's suggested projects at least provide some choice, another important feature of effective writing assignments.

In addition, each task Maura suggests would require students to revisit scenes and details in the play, not only a worthwhile task for a richer experience of a Shakespearean play, but also a good scaffolding tool to prepare for exams in which students need to cite "specific textual evidence" (NYS Reading Standard CCR.1). Engaging intellectual exercises like this would simulate the skills required for high-stakes tests without slogging through yet another practice test from a past year.

Finally, together we might brainstorm ways in which Maura's creative assignments could be tweaked so that they *were* aimed at readers outside the class. Her idea regarding Yorick's talking skull might result in a play that could be performed for the class or the school. There are a number of real-world outlets for plays, even those written by young people. For example, the publication *Figment* publishes plays and other genres written by writers 13 years old and up. *The New York Times* and other organizations frequently publish lists of where college- or school-aged writers can publish. Maura's suggested assignments to explore Horatio's true feelings could be shared with the real world in several ways: a film uploaded to YouTube, a recording made into a public podcast, or a piece of writing submitted to venues open to student writing, depending on what the school district permits, of course. Hamlet's imagined letter of apology to Ophelia might be developed into a quirky take on an academic essay or even a humor piece. Both Scholastic Classroom Magazines and the National Council of Teachers of English sponsor contests that solicit different genres written by teens, as does *Teen Ink*. Not only do these publications offer new audiences for students' work, but they can motivate students to revise and edit their work to increase their chances of getting published, honing their piece to fit the genre, the publication style, and the needs of the specific readership. What's more, most of these student-focused outlets provide samples of previous publications by teens, which can function as "mentor texts" (Robb, 2010) or "framing texts" (Dean, 2003) and which students simply can enjoy or can use as models. Students can study these sample texts for ideas regarding topics, length, voice, register, vocabulary level, sentence structure, and so on. Some of these online venues, such as *The Artifice* (for people over 18), publish literary analyses and even offer peer review and revision opportunities.

What I learned, therefore, from off-topic representations is to mine them for clues to the honest doubts my students may have regarding the same course content that excites me. I'm so enthusiastic about these writing practices we read about in this class that I can miss students' skepticism about those same practices. Sketches like Maura's, outliers that they are, force me to reflect. They provide opportunities to launch discussions that would tie the best ideas from such drawings to more challenging writing projects. Although in the past I would not have started a discussion on authentic writing by using *Hamlet*, I may well do that from now on. This sketch taught me that I can take better advantage of my students' interests in literary texts to teach them what I want them to know about making writing more empowering for their students.

Sketches like those foregrounded in this chapter function as excellent formative assessments. They are windows to students' misunderstandings and doubts. They can help teachers realize what threshold concepts need to be recast, or what troublesome knowledge is counterintuitive to students' previous beliefs or assumptions. The insights learned from these sketches, if gained early enough, can help teachers regroup for remaining classes in the semester, or reflect on ways to make the next semester address complex concepts in a more effective way.

CHAPTER 4

Grappling With Traditional Versus Contemporary/Critical Theory

I occasionally teach a graduate class on the teaching of literature, designed for new graduate students who soon will be instructors themselves. This course is meant to help these future teachers become more aware of the critical/interpretive lenses they are using and to think through how those lenses might shape pedagogy. To help students grapple with different critical and interpretive theories, I have students juxtapose traditional literary criticism to poststructuralist approaches. For example, new criticism might be juxtaposed visually against queer theory, feminism, critical race theory, new historicism, disability studies, or other poststructuralist approaches. A number of resulting contrasted representations were particularly instructive in helping students see important differences between these theories and how those differences might affect their future students' engagement with reading and even students' sense of identity and self-esteem—all issues related to inclusion and/or access.

In this class, we read about student-centered classroom practices, active learning, ways to improve class participation and discussion, factors affecting texts chosen for a class, trigger warnings, the canon controversy, workload, syllabus and assignment construction, assessment, and a host of other topics that people serious about teaching need to consider, including the availability of audio texts versus print texts.

We also spent time on literary and critical theory. I wanted to make sure students understood how these theories manifest in teaching: in the selection of texts, in the questions posed (or not posed) about those texts, and in projects and assessments designed around them. We read selections from Richter's *Falling Into Theory* (1994), background on Matthew Arnold's (1869) view of literature, Sharon Crowley and Debra Hawhee's (1998) critique of Arnoldian humanism, Fahnestock and Secor's (1991) essay "The Rhetoric of Literary Criticism," Henry Louis Gates's (1989/1994) essay on canon formation, Mitchell and Snyder's (2000) work on "narrative prosthesis" in disability studies, and numerous other essays explaining or demonstrating a variety of theoretical approaches to reading texts and some consequences of those theories.

Students are usually pretty good at verbally describing these different approaches, but I want them to think more deeply and metaphorically about how these theories shape our pedagogies. Every question posed about a text in an English class has a theory underpinning it, whether or not the questioner is aware of that theory. I want students to be aware and to make conscious choices. Having them produce JVRs can help them do that.

TEXT-AS-SHOE METAPHOR

Whenever I review traditional and poststructuralist theories, I bring in a high-heeled shoe. I place the shoe on the portable classroom podium, which I usually keep on the floor in the corner of the room but have moved, for this purpose, to my desk. So the shoe, sitting on the podium, which is on the desk, is now high enough for everyone to see. I let it sit there for a beat. Then I pose a series of questions to the class, using the shoe as a stand-in for a novel, poem, play, or other literary text that is the target of our interpretive or critical framework. I ask, "What kinds of questions might a new critic, or structuralist, pose?" If no one answers, I will: What is the structure of the shoe? What kind of a shoe is it? What category of "shoe" does it fit into? To what extent is it a work of art? Or, What makes it worthy of being called a "shoe"? Students know that the new critical movement was a reaction against biographical criticism, so the discussion now turns to what questions these new critics would *not* ask: Who made it? Where were they from? Where did they live?

Then I ask what Marxist critics might ask about the shoe. By now, students get into this analogy and someone usually replies that Marxist critics would ask about the means of production of the shoe, whose labor produced it, who profits from its sale, and so on. Does this product resist or perpetuate questionable aspects of the status quo? Which group's values are inscribed in this product—explicitly or implicitly? Does this product resist or perpetuate questionable aspects of the status quo?

From there we move on to biographical criticism: What are some biographical facts about the designer of this product? Could some of those factors have influenced the design of this product? Reader response critics might ask: Have you ever had any experience with a product like this? Have you ever worn a shoe like this? Under what circumstances? Do you know someone who has? How does wearing (or watching someone wear) this shoe make you feel? What would you do if you were in a situation where you (or a loved one) had to wear this shoe? How might your prior experience with shoes—or with shoes like this—influence your impression of this shoe?

Once we're on a roll with these hypothetical questions, it's easy to keep it going. Postcolonial critics might ask: In what ways does this shoe reflect the culture in which it appears? In what ways does this shoe—or the culture of which it is a part—impose one set of cultural values over another set of cultural values? This shoe has "universal" appeal—true or false? Feminist or gender studies critics might ask: What role does gender play in who uses this product? Which groups benefit from the use of this product? Which groups are harmed, or at least do not benefit, from the use of this product? What larger questions about gender and society does this shoe raise—explicitly or because of the assumptions it seems to reflect regarding gender and society? What does this item—and its intended use—teach us about the society in which it plays a part? To what extent does this product resist or perpetuate questionable aspects of the status quo? Then we move on to queer theory, critical race theory, disability studies, psychoanalytic criticism, and so on. Without going into the nuances of these different approaches, students get a good review and/or insights about these theories. At least two students mentioned to me in comments later that this shoe discussion helped them conceptualize their sketch.

After some readings, my shoe demonstration, and our discussion of how critical frameworks shape questions, I also show them my own sketch regarding literary/critical theories: a text up on a pedestal versus texts being cheered by students or students being crushed by the texts. (See Figure 1.1 for this sketch and an explanation of it.) It is after this "shoe literature theory" discussion that I ask them to sketch a JVR juxtaposing some different interpretive or critical approaches to theory. Students do several practice sketching sessions throughout the semester, always linked to a group of readings or a lively issue we've just discussed.

READERS' AWARENESS OF LENSES

After this preparation work, students can choose any controversy from class to represent in a sketch for their last reading response project, worth 5% of the class grade. Several people chose to juxtapose issues related to theory. Figure 4.1 shows Ella's juxtaposition of not just different lenses, but people's different levels of awareness regarding those lenses.

Here is Ella's written description:

> My visual represents two different approaches to theory in literature
> classes. This image was inspired by my nearsightedness, and the
> fact that when I am wearing glasses, I am accustomed to them and
> unaware of their presence. The image on the left suggests that the
> same thing can happen with the theoretical lenses (see what I did
> there) through which we view literature. In this image, the thin
> border signifies the frame being used to discuss the text. This frame
> is unobtrusive. It does not draw attention to itself, and it is possible

Figure 4.1. Ella's JVR of Different Approaches to Literary Theory: Being Unaware Versus Being Aware

Two juxtaposed images. On the left is an open book, which takes up most of the frame. There is a thin black line, a border, that frames the page on which the book is drawn. The thin black line is hardly noticeable. On the right, that same book is present, but it is much smaller and is positioned near the top of the page. There are four pairs of glasses on the page, each with different-shaped lenses. There is no thin border around the page.

to forget or ignore that we are looking at the book through a lens because the focus is on the text. While the theory is present, it is in the periphery and largely overlooked. The image on the right signifies a different approach, where instructors draw attention to the theory they are using. In this image, the different glasses represent different theoretical approaches, and their presence in the image draws attention to the lenses we use when we interpret literature. It also suggests that in teaching students about different theoretical approaches (instead of naturalizing and automatizing one), students can take off and put on different lenses, experiencing a different view and developing a different understanding of the text.

I must admit that the first time I saw Ella's images, I did not even notice the thin border she points out in her explanation. In my defense, I was looking at about 15 of these that night and not really studying them. Also, my own visual literacy is not that acute. However, this failure of mine to see that frame, of course, proves her point: Sometimes, in a literature class, instructors and students just start doing things automatically with a text. We may start looking for evidence of themes, character arcs, conflicts, metaphors, and so on, with an assumed purpose of understanding the text's meaning or appreciating its brilliance. This decision regarding which elements in the text to analyze, if it is thought of at all, seems to have been made long ago and far away by unknown powers who are not to be questioned. Or the ritual of discussing certain "literary elements" seems not to have been a decision at all, but just is.

The thin line around that left side of the sketch is probably the traditional new critical lens, which does center the text as the thing-to-be-analyzed and further requires that it be a certain kind of rich text, of course, with several levels of meaning that emerge upon "close reading" and analysis by certain kinds of readers. In the high school and college classes I've observed through the years, this new critical–influenced lens typically is not pointed out to students. The questions posed simply initiate a new critical analysis without naming it as such. Note that in Ella's sketch on the left, no one points to or even notices the thin line, the lens that is being used to frame how students will discuss the text. Poststructuralist critics would, of course, not only point out that thin frame, they probably would critique it for its lack of self-awareness or at least for how it seems to discourage theoretical awareness in many people who employ it as a framework. (I almost want to combine my sketch with Ella's and to insert a gleeful stick figure on the right side of our combined sketches who points, triumphantly, to the thin frame around the book on the left, forcing the adoring stick figures worshiping the book on the pedestal to examine that frame.) By extending discussion of these simple sketches, sometimes even comparing them with one another, often we further analyze important issues from the semester so far. These drawings help us review and revisit concepts and controversies.

PRINT VERSUS AUDIO TEXTS

Another topic we read and talk about in this class for future instructors of literature is audio texts. First, I remind students that they should make sure the texts they order for a class are also available digitally, for readers who need to enlarge the font, and via audio, for readers who need to listen to a text. We discuss questions such as these: For readers who can choose either mode, how does reading a text with eyes differ from reading with ears? What advantages and drawbacks does print offer? What are some advantages and disadvantages of audio text, including the hardware and software involved? Contrasting print and audio modes was the subject of Jon's visual representation, shown in Figure 4.2. The left side of his pencil sketch depicts someone reading and what that reader imagined in his mind. The right side shows a reader listening to a book as well as what was going through his thoughts as he did so. What these two readers imagined was quite different.

Here is Jon's explanation of his visual representation:

> In these two panels, I have attempted to depict two different experiences of reading a text. The experience of reading a physical book is shown in the left panel, and in the right, I have portrayed how this experience contrasts with that of listening to an audio book. The scene I'm reading/illustrating is from Chapter 22 of Charlotte Brontë's

Figure 4.2. Jon's JVR of Reading a Text Versus Listening to a Text

Two juxtaposed scenes. In the left one, in the lower left corner, a man is seen reading a book. In the background, a nun walks down a hallway. In the right one, in the lower right corner, a man is seen wearing headphones, apparently listening to an audio book. There are six smaller scene depictions of what the man is visualizing: a close-up of a shoe clicking on the floor, with a young woman's face being startled at what she sees. Then she runs toward a door. Then we see stairs that she runs down and we see her raised hands as she tells people what she saw. Then we see her weeping at a desk, crying, "My letter!" Then we see a hand giving an envelope back to two other hands.

Villette, in which the protagonist Lucy Snowe first encounters the ghostly image of a nun in the garret at the school where she works.

To illustrate the left panel, I read this scene, imagined what it looked like, and then drew the image that I had recreated in my mind. This process, and the image that it produced, mirrors the experience of reading a physical text in the sense that I was able to pause, reflect, and examine the language that Brontë uses to describe the scene before I ever set pencil to paper. In the 10 minutes or so that I spent on this illustration, I only read about three sentences from the novel itself. I was able to focus on this short passage as reading a physical book is conducive to a kind of "slow" reading.

In the second panel, I was not able to reflect as much on the text, as audio books are less conducive to this type of reading. However, I found that I was able to portray a significant amount more information regarding the narrative of this chapter, and I even picked up on details that I had not noticed as much when reading the physical book. These aspects are reflected in my illustrations, which—rather than focusing on a single moment—depict the events of nearly half the chapter (which is what I was able to hear in the 10 minutes of my audio book listening). Thus, in addition to seeing the nun, Lucy hears the creak of a footstep, screams in fright, rushes to the door, descends the stairs to find her employer, cries out to Madame Beck that there is an intruder in the garret, rushes back to the garret as she remembers that she has left her letter there, mourns over the loss of this letter (which has mysteriously disappeared), and then rejoices when the letter is returned to her. These illustrations are a little sloppier than my first one, and I think that even this reflects how these two experiences differ. While reading a physical text allowed me to reflect and read slowly, better developing my own thoughts in response to the scene, listening to an audio book helped me to keep moving along, covering more ground and picking up on details that I otherwise might have not noticed.

As we can see, and as Jon described it, the physical text, for him, provided what he calls a "slow" reading, in which he was able to "pause, reflect, and examine the language" the author used in just about three sentences of the text. The scene on the right, where he listens to the book, shows many more events in the sequence of the narrative and represents almost half a chapter, what he said he heard in about 10 minutes of listening. In his view, "the physical text allowed me to reflect and read slowly, better developing my own thoughts in response to the scene. . . ." The audio book "helped me to keep moving along, covering more ground and picking up on details that I otherwise might have not noticed."

Jon did this reading response as a kind of experiment. He recounts how much of the scene he read, "about three sentences," and then sketched what he imagined as he read it. Then he listened to the same section, which covered about 10 minutes of listening, which was almost half the chapter, and then sketched out what he imagined. In my classes in which teaching literature is foregrounded, students frequently debate the pros and cons of audio texts versus print texts. Many of these English majors say that they greatly prefer eyes-on-page reading, and I sometimes detect some general disapproval of audio texts, as if listening to them is not "really" reading. Jon's sketch is an attempt to represent each experience as honestly as he can, reporting what he noticed while reading in each mode. His juxtaposed scenes would be a good opportunity to open a conversation regarding how literature instructors might incorporate both ways of reading into their classes. It also might encourage more research into what studies or surveys might have been done on this topic, to help new teachers and their students take the best advantage of reading in all its forms. Jon's JVR opened a productive discussion of not only the pros and cons of each platform, but how audio texts can provide access for a larger percentage of students who, for a variety of reasons, may not be able to read using their eyes or who comprehend better through hearing a text.

PROBLEMATIC CANONICAL TEXTS

A major project in this class on the teaching of college literature was to do an analysis of how canonical texts were being discussed in schools and colleges. One way to access some of this information is to google, for example, "discussion questions on *The Glass Menagerie*" or on whatever text one chooses. Teachers, college instructors, and publishers often post such questions, and often "themes" to discuss and, occasionally, suggested "answers" to their questions.

Because I wanted these future English instructors to be critically conscious of the approaches to interpretation and analysis that they were using themselves and that they would be using in their courses, I designed a short project I thought would help them develop this insight. First, they were to choose a literary text they thought they'd teach one day, and then they were to research how that particular literary text had been discussed in classes. I asked them to find out: What "study questions," "discussion questions," or even syllabi, student papers, quizzes, or other reception documents frame how this text has been used in college literature classes? What interpretive lenses do the writers of these questions seem to be using? How do you know? What assumptions do the writers of these questions seem to be making about the purpose of literature? About the purpose of reading this text in a class? What makes you say so? What do you think of the questions you're finding and the assumptions upon which they seem to be based? What would you keep, discard, or add? Why?

To give them a sense of what this project would be like, we of course practiced some of this analysis in class. We'd look at some "study questions" or "discussion questions" we could find online about a canonical text, and then we'd try to deduce what literary or critical lens the question writer seemed to be using as a framework. For example, questions about readers' reactions to a text were most likely a result of a "reader response" approach. Questions about depictions of women might come from feminist theory. Questions about structure and symbols might come out of new critical traditions, and so on. I also had students read snippets from my book, *Disabling Characters: Representations of Disability in Young Adult Literature* (2015), in which I analyze groups of discussion questions I found online regarding young adult novels that featured protagonists with disabilities. Students in this class, therefore, had been steeped not only in readings and discussions about controversies surrounding canonical literature, but in questions about the questions posed about literature: what those questions were designed to do and how those questions might perpetuate stereotypes about underrepresented groups, as well as what alternative questions might challenge harmful stereotypes present in canonical and other texts.

Challenging Stereotypes in the Canon

Angela took up some of these issues in her juxtaposed visual representation, in which she used an analogy to show different ways of handling canonical texts, especially problematic ones that contained, for example, stereotypes about women, people of color, people with disabilities, and so forth. As shown in Figure 4.3, she starts with a dilapidated barn.

Here is Angela's explanation:

> Each side of my visual representation is a metaphor for a different way of dealing with canonical texts. There is a problem with the ways in which canonical texts are taught; that is part of the reason why we are analyzing discussion questions. Accordingly, the first image in both sides, left and right, is the same: a broken-down barn with a person standing in front of it. In both cases, the person sees how broken the barn is, and understands how irresponsible it would be to use the barn in its current state. But the story shifts between left and right: On the left, the person goes to the hardware store to buy supplies in order to fix up the barn. We see the person fixing the roof in the next panel. Finally, on the bottom, the barn is completely renovated and is now a venue for hosting community events, such as the dinner party in the last panel. Lights hang on either side to represent a brighter and more

Figure 4.3. Angela's JVR Contrasting Different Ways of Handling Problematic Canonical Texts

Two juxtaposed sets of cartoon panels. On the left side, the top panel shows a figure looking at a dilapidated barn. The middle panel on this side shows the figure using tools and labor to renovate the barn. The bottom panel shows the barn all fixed up and people happily using it for community gatherings. On the right side, the top panel shows the same figure looking at the same dilapidated barn. In the middle panel, the figure drives a bulldozer, which knocks the barn down. In the bottom panel, trees and deer now occupy the space formally taken up by the dilapidated barn.

welcoming atmosphere. On the right, the person has decided that the work of fixing the barn outweighs the good it will do, so they tear down the barn with a bulldozer and plant a forest in its place. In the final panel, we see deer roaming through the trees.

On both sides, the barn is no longer what it once was; the person on the left, who renovates the barn, makes something new out of it that will best serve the community: a space for people to come together. This represents the point of view that we can continue using canonical texts, but we need to drastically change the way that we do so. On the right, the person has dismantled the barn completely, representing the point of view that many canonical texts are beyond the point where they can be made useful and must be completely discarded in order to heal the damage that their presence causes.

I wanted to make each choice look more or less as favorable as the other; in both cases, the barn is broken and needs to be fixed. However, the possibilities are somewhat mutually exclusive. Canonical texts cannot be simultaneously used and not used; the barn must be fixed or torn down. I wanted my visual representation to show the validity of the opinions on both sides, as well as the conflict between the two strategies.

Angela's contrasted scenes have no words in them, but her drawings are clear enough for us to see that on the left side the old barn is being fixed up, and on the right it is being torn down. She's right that there's no apparent judgment on the cartoonist's part that one way—renovation or razing—is better than the other. There's also no debate about the condition of the barn at the beginning. Clearly it is dilapidated and dangerous.

In this analogy, Angela suggests the danger of canonical texts that contain harmful stereotypes or tired narratives about different groups of people. Like the old barn, old texts can pose potential problems, especially, perhaps, to people who enter the barn by habit without noticing that it's falling down, or people who study a book in class year after year without realizing how its depictions or assumptions about some characters might be harmful to real readers. Someone needs to make a decision about what to do about the old barn, or the old texts. Fixing up the barn so that it can continue to be used without harming anyone is analogous to an instructor posing more critical questions about a problematic text.

For example, "What are we to think of Hemingway's depiction of women in some of his novels?" Or, for *Macbeth*, "Why is it that so many online 'discussion questions' about Lady Macbeth seem to depict her as more evil than her husband?" Or, for *Of Mice and Men*, "What might be some real-life consequences of depicting Lennie as someone who is dangerous and who is shot by his friend at the end? What message might that send about real people with intellectual disabilities?" Problematizing aspects of a canonical text is different from simply trying to determine its meaning. Fixing up the old barn in order to keep using it is analogous to framing a discussion of a canonical text so that whatever harmful or questionable assumptions it seems to be promoting might be rendered less harmful. The barn, or the text, can still be enjoyed, but not without some substantial work by the barn's owner, or the instructor assigning the text.

Some barn owners, however, might decide that the building is too far gone to salvage—that it's better to just knock it down. Similarly, some English instructors might decide that a canonical text supports one too many racist, misogynist, or ablest views of the world to continue to use it in class, despite whatever literary merits it was thought to have through the years. Those instructors might decide to take that text off their reading list and replace it with something else, like the pristine forest once the old barn was knocked down. Angela's insightful juxtaposition of these two possibilities provides a good point of departure for new teachers to grapple with this issue. She begins with the premise that some canonical texts must be dealt with one way or the other. Her sketches can help people discuss different options. Recently, there have been lively and far-reaching Twitter discussions with the hashtag #DisruptTexts, led by Tricia Ebarvia, Lorena German, Kimberly N. Parker, and Julia E. Torres (n.d.), who argue not only that racist canonical texts should be disrupted and problematized, but that different texts should be added to the curriculum to help transform a society that often holds back students of color. As mentioned earlier, these authors also have a #DisruptTexts website. And they've written separately about these issues as well.

Expanding the Canon

Another student from that same class who took up the canon controversy was Vivien. She was responding to an article we read by Annette Portillo (2013), who argues in *The CEA Forum* that American literature courses should include texts focusing on Native American literature and culture. Vivien's representation juxtaposes one class that is "Staying Close to the Traditional Western Canon" to one that is "Including Voices From Other Cultures (Annette Portillo Article)" (see Figure 4.4).

Here is Vivien's description:

> The sketch on the left shows a teacher who hardly strays outside the traditional Western canon. As a result the students' world is limited, with the potential that anyone outside can be othered, misunderstood, stereotyped, unfamiliar, exoticized, or seen as uncultured.
>
> On the right is a class taught by a teacher who includes the literary processes of other cultures in her syllabus. In this case, the class has read books mentioned in Annette Portillo's article. The choice to include readings which broaden the canon, can provide students with a deeper understanding of, and empathy for, individuals and groups outside their own culture.

Upon closer examination, there are other features worth discussing in Vivien's contrasting scenes. First, we might add more information about the texts she lists briefly, which are explained further in the Annette Portillo (2013) article she references. *The New Mestiza* refers to Chicana scholar Gloria E. Anzaldúa's 1987 text, *Borderlands/La Frontera. Man Made of Words* is Pulitzer Prize–winning Native American writer M. Scott Momaday's 1997 collection of essays, stories, and passages. "Yellow Woman" (1974) is a short story by Leslie Marmon Silko, who grew up on a Native American reservation, Laguna Pueblo, in New Mexico. *American Indian*

Figure 4.4. Vivien's JVR Depicting the Traditional Canon Versus a More Representative Canon

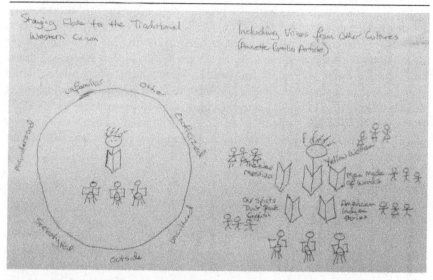

Two juxtaposed sketches. The one on the left is labeled "Staying Close to the Traditional Western Canon." Drawn inside a large circle are four stick figures. There is a teacher with a large book opened. Three smaller figures, students, sit at desks. Surrounding the circle are seven words: unfamiliar, other, exoticized, uncultured, outside, stereotyped, and misunderstood. The sketch on the right is labeled "Including Voices From Other Cultures (Annette Portillo Article)." The same teacher has a book open, but now there are other large books open as well, and there are three students at desks, but also five other trios of students, each group standing together, with their arms out. Next to each group is the name of a short story, book, or documentary, respectively: "Yellow Woman," *Man Made of Words, American Indian Stories, The New Mestiza,* and *Our Spirits Don't Speak English.*

Stories is a 1921 collection by Zitkala-Sa (Gertrude Bonnin), a Dakota Sioux Indian. *Our Spirits Don't Speak English* is a 2008 documentary film about an Indian boarding school. Not only is Vivien's sketch a good review of Portillo's article; it reminds the future college literature instructors in this class what texts they might add to their readings when designing an American literature class.

It's also clear from Vivien's contrasting scenes that she believes the canon should be more inclusive, and her sketches are a visual argument supporting that belief. First, not only are the rich texts mentioned in the "Voices From Other Cultures" side excluded from the "Traditional Western Canon" side, but the students reading the Western canon are not even aware of what is being excluded. They all seem to be reading just one book. They are isolated inside a closed circle, without access to, or knowledge of, the voices and stories outside of their enclosure. The words outside their circle are just words indicating exclusion ("unfamiliar," "uncultured," "misunderstood," etc.). There are no titles or authors associated with them. Also, there are literally many fewer stick figures on the Western canon side because the "other," "exoticized" words do not have people associated with them. They are just words. In contrast, the inclusive, multicultural side shows not one book, but five. The titles of the works are provided, and each book is surrounded by three stick figures, some men, some women. There is no circular barrier around the students. They can see, name, and interact with the "voices from other cultures." Finally, most of the stick figures on this side have arms, while those on the "Western canon" side do not. It's possible Vivien simply ran out of time, and the dearth of arms on this side is a minor detail. However, the stick people's lack of arms might suggest that they are a passive, captive audience within their cordoned-off classroom, lacking agency and powerless to choose among a variety of stories, cultures, and protagonists. The "other cultures" side has 15 more stick figures—with arms—and more books. Even without Vivien's written explanation, her contrasting scenes make a strong case for a more inclusive literary canon.

The contrasted sketches from this course bring us instantly to the crux of important debates today about what students should read in school, how they should read it, and what questions are important in discussing these texts. Books, articles, and discussions can do that, too. But sketches can show us in an instant what's at stake and also show us the stakeholders. They can function as visual rhetoric, making the case for the position taken by the sketcher. And they can help us introduce or return to critical issues we need to address further, putting all of us on the same page to see those issues at the same time, a visual point of departure that provokes more discussion.

CHAPTER 5

Sketching as a Tool for Reorganization

Juxtaposed visual representations are also useful in helping writers reorganize their drafts or identify problems they may be having as they work toward a finished project. Some drawings in this chapter are examples of how students juxtaposed a quick sketch of their draft's current organization to that of a hypothetical, alternative organization. Others visually represented a problem they needed to solve in their early draft and juxtaposed it to a visual representation of how they might solve it. Sometimes this quick flyover of two different plans can help writers generate a better way to structure their argument or make it stronger. The effort needed in this task to identify, sketch, and try to solve a problem in a draft sometimes can reveal a possible solution. Even if the JVR itself does not produce a helpful insight for revision, sometimes the discussion of other students' JVRs during this activity does spark an insight for improvement.

Students produced these contrasted sketches to help troubleshoot issues in writing and to plan revisions for their major writing projects, which were drafted at this point but not finished. I had used visual representation for this purpose earlier in my career with some success (see Chapter 3 of *Talking, Sketching, Moving* [2001], available as a downloadable free sample from the publisher), so in this chapter I'll describe recent examples of students using this tool. That a number of my students found this quick sketching helpful suggests that a similar activity may help other writers. The visual representations in this chapter were drawn quickly during class time and were not intended to be communicative devices for a large audience, or even a fixed blueprint for a definite revision by their creator. Some are more metaphoric than linear. They are rough, simple drawings, highly individualized. They represent, for one person, where their draft is at one moment in time and how that draft's structure might be adjusted or a problem addressed. These JVRs were not graded.

JUXTAPOSING TO TROUBLESHOOT

By the time students did the sketches described in this chapter, they had already done several JVRs in class to help explore abstract concepts or to better understand complex controversies in the field. Therefore, the request to sketch something was no longer brand-new to them. However, this time the task required them to think abstractly and holistically about their writing projects, to imagine a bird's-eye view of the current structure and then to imagine a different structure. They also could visually represent a problem and a proposed solution. I do this activity once I know that all students have a working draft of a major writing project for the class, which is always due late in the semester. I also make sure they have at least 1 week left in which they can revise or rework their project, should they choose to after this sketching exercise.

I give similar directions to all my classes, so one narrative of the process should suffice to explain the context for the five classes studied in this project. (I plan to adapt this process for online classes.) Students had a major writing project due in a week, but they had been working on it for a good part of the semester and had already received feedback on their drafts from a small group of peers, and some students had received feedback from me. They were required to post their developing papers on our class Blackboard site, so I knew they all had a draft, not just an outline. I asked them to bring a hard copy or e-copy to class that night. Once class was under way, I told them they would be creating juxtaposed visual representations again, two sketches, one on either side of a divided piece of paper. I gave them a choice of situations, or combinations thereof, they might juxtapose visually:

1. The current organization of their paper, contrasted with a possible alternative way to organize a revised version
2. A problem in their paper that needed to be solved, contrasted with a way to solve it

They sketched for about 10 minutes. In the beginning of this activity, I showed them a sketch I did earlier in the day with one of my other classes, demonstrating an organizational problem I was having with my own writing project at that time. I always show students my primitive attempts so that they can focus not on any anxiety they may feel about their perceived lack of drawing skills, but rather on their ideas.

One student in this class, Shauna, added to this preparatory discussion about major revision and visualization to say that sometimes she literally cuts her papers up and rearranges the parts to help better organize them. Shauna's comment, therefore, was a good lead-in to this JVR exercise because the physical manipulation of text segments is also a way to reconceptualize organization or other issues without combing through all 15 or so pages of a draft.

As the students worked on their visual representations, I looked to see who was finished and asked them whether I could take a photo of their sketch with my tablet, and whether I could project it. Some said yes, some said no. If time permits, I have students explain their sketch to each other in pairs or very small groups; this allows everyone to describe their own drawings out loud and to see what someone else has done.

I also asked them to write a few sentences explaining their contrasting sketches, and some explained them orally. Several people generously volunteered to show their work to the entire class. I forced no one and I explained up front that these classroom-generated sketches are not graded in any way. We could not devote the whole class session to this activity, but we spent about 45 minutes talking about several students' visual representations, which I projected for all to see. They were produced as a fast way for the individuals doing the sketching to conceptualize their projects thus far, how those projects were organized, and how they might tweak that arrangement to best effect. The sketching, plus the discussion of the projected sketches, took about an hour of class time.

Old Versus New Organization

One projected JVR from that class, shown in Figure 5.1, sparked some discussion, with at least one other student saying she found that the suggested changes were also applicable to her own paper. In this sketch, Shae juxtaposes her current and possible new organization for her major project entitled "Standard American English: A Fair Assessment Tool?"

As seen on the left, in her current organization, Shae starts with a rant, then provides a history of Standard American English, a tour taking up a large chunk of her draft, the details of which could begin to dampen readers' interest. Only then does she bring in expert opinions on the topic, then makes her way to a conclusion. Nowhere does she explore the critical controversy surrounding this issue. The proposed organization on the right is quite different. She meant for this to be read from the bottom up, with the wide bottom of the triangle representing the start of the paper, and the conclusion (top of pyramid) at the end. However, in this new version on the right, she introduces the controversy right after the background, going through the pros and cons of her issue, as well as recent developments, before reaching the conclusion.

When she first showed this to the class, the sketch on the right started with "background info" (reading from the bottom up). I went up to the screen, pointed to that section, and suggested that she wouldn't need to start with just background—that she could add a teaser of the controversy early on. Before she handed in her sketch later, she had added the "teaser: controversy," shown in the sketch, as coming first. In the discussion following this projection, others said they found this idea useful for their revisions, too. Shae mentioned that she had added "teaser: controversy" to start the essay after her initial drawing and after we had talked about how too much background could weigh down the paper. In the revised, final version of her

Figure 5.1. Shae's Old and New Structure for Her Writing Project

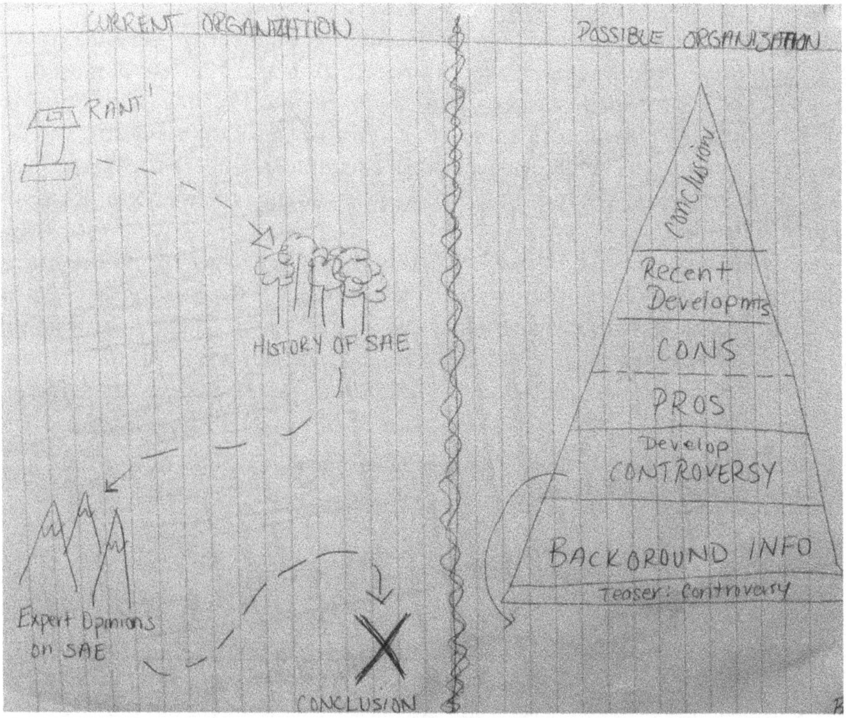

Two juxtaposed organizational patterns, with "Current Organization" on the left and "Possible Organization" on the right. On the left, "rant" is at the top, with a broken arrow going to "history of SAE," then lines to mountains that say, "expert opinions on SAE," and then an X at "conclusion." On the right is a pyramid. The paper starts at the bottom with "teaser: controversy," then above that "background info," then "develop controversy," then "pros," then "cons," then "recent developments," and "conclusion" at the very top of the pyramid.

paper, Shae did indeed begin with a teaser to get readers' attention and then moved into the background of the language controversy she was exploring.

In the end-of-semester surveys, when asked about the usefulness of doing the drawings of her organization, Shae checked "Helped a lot." She wrote, "After the visual representation activity, I was able to organize my paper following the image I had drawn. Previously, I had to be just writing to write and get the information out of my head and onto the 'paper.'" To Question 7, which asked about whether the discussions of the JVRs were helpful, Shae wrote: "Having to discuss the visualization helped to clarify parts of the drawing in relation to issues I had with organization. I was able to gain insight about issues I did not realize I was having yet had drawn for the assignment."

Problem Versus Proposed Solution

The value in these representations is not only that each person has the opportunity to think broadly about overall organization and alternative patterns, a quick and useful intellectual exercise by itself, but that the discussion of other people's problems and solutions often can spark an insight in listeners, when their own sketch, by itself, is not terribly useful for them, and can help them see where they too might be able to change their organization to improve their papers.

For example, it was Ella's sketch (Figure 5.2) that generated the most discussion in this class, with students saying it hit a nerve regarding their own problems with many academic papers they write. Hers was not an organizational issue but a "Problem Versus Proposed Solution" depiction. Ella's sketch on the left illustrates a common problem in students' papers:

Figure 5.2. Ella's JVR of a Problem With Her Paper: Too Many Critics Having Too Much Voice in Her Project

Two juxtaposed sketches. On the left, seven stick figures have speech bubbles. All are labeled "critic," except for one, which is labeled "me." The "me" figure is substantially smaller than the "critics." On the right, the "me" figure is now bigger than the "critics," with a much bigger speech bubble, and there are only four "critics," instead of six.

too many critics saying too much, drowning out the "me" voice of the student writer, the little figure in the middle of the left sketch.

Ella explained that in her revised paper, she wanted her voice to be more prominent than all the critics she was using in her current version. Several students nodded their heads at this problem, recognizing a common one in student writing: the preponderance of critics' voices overwhelming the voice of the student writer. They said Ella's sketch inspired them to revisit their drafts and see whether they could mitigate that problem in their own papers.

The point of Ella's sketch was this: Make sure the critics or experts in your paper don't drown out your voice. Why not simply give students that advice orally or in writing? Or why not simply have Ella talk about her worry that the other voices are taking over her draft? It's beyond the scope of this project to measure the effects of written/verbal advice regarding author's voice versus a visual representation of this common problem. But we know that seeing a problem represented visually, next to a sketch of the problem solved, may be more likely to stick in people's heads than if they merely read or hear advice regarding it. Creating a visual can spark insights; seeing one's own or someone else's visual can be a memory aid. No one wants to be the little stick-figure "me" whose voice is lost in a sea of pontificating critics. It's empowering, however, to envision the larger "me" figure with a more prominent voice on the right side of the JVR. It's also possible that being asked to *sketch* a problem she was having helped Ella to identify it as an issue in the first place. I had an opportunity to see and respond to Ella's early draft and, of course, I saw the final version. While other people's quotes and views dominate the beginning of her first draft, her final draft begins with a brief quote but then is followed by Ella's own introduction and description of what her paper will do. The rest of her paper is well-balanced and engaging, with critics used for emphasis but her own argument leading us through her analysis. It's possible that my consult with her about her early draft may have influenced her rethinking of how to use critics, but the JVR also may have helped cement her decisions as she revised her work.

VIEWING VERSUS DISCUSSING

Regardless of how much influence Ella's JVR may have had on her own revision plan, her oral explanation of her JVR surely helped other students recognize, and perhaps begin to solve, a similar problem in their projects. In these few minutes of class time, students saw these contrasted images, heard the problem (of too many yammering critics) described, and could contribute actively to the discussion—a multimodal learning activity.

Bringing attention to this issue in this multimodal format, with Ella's different-sized figures and speech balloons in her juxtaposed sketches, as well as her verbal explanation, may be a more accessible way to help students pay more attention to this issue as they put finishing touches on their drafts. It is also the combination of activities associated with the drawings that may be particularly inclusive, either because the information comes through a variety of senses, or because different modes affect people differently. The active learning component also may play a part: students speaking and listening during the discussion following Ella's explanation of her sketch. According to students' comments about the JVRs, some found creating the drawing itself useful but the discussion less so. Others said that doing the sketches themselves did not help them much, but that the discussion that followed did.

Feedback on Surveys

In Question 6 of the surveys I gave at the end of the semester, I asked whether the JVRs on their drafts were helpful. Ella checked the "Helped a little" box and wrote this:

> As is true of many graduate students, I tend to rely too much on quotes from my sources and not enough on my own voice. I know this is a problem, but the visual representation allowed me to see why.

For Question 7, which asked about whether the discussion that followed the drawing was helpful, Ella again checked "Helped a little." But she added, "I found that thinking through the visual representation and then drawing it was more helpful than discussing it afterward." For Ella, it was the act of sketching itself that helped her zero in on her paper's problem and solution.

Other students, however, had the reverse reaction. A student in the same class, Rosheena, found that the discussion of these several JVRs really helped her, more so than the sketching itself. In the survey, Rosheena checked "Didn't help at all" to Question 6 about the actual sketching. But she checked "Helped a lot" to Question 7 about the usefulness of the discussion following the sketching:

> So for me, my own visual representation confused me but that's because I was already in my own head about my paper. However, when I saw other people's I felt so much better because their visual representations cleared my mind and gave me alot [sic] of insight on how to restructure my paper in order to organize it in a good way, also specifically Ella's visual representation helped me understand how I was seeing myself in the context of my essay as the "supposedly" main voice in the paper.

We see, then, that Ella's thinking about how to represent her problems, and then actually sketching it, did help Ella, but her oral explanation did not. In contrast, Rosheena said that her own sketch did not help her, but that Ella's sketch and explanation did. It's important, therefore, when doing these JVRs, to build in time for some projections and discussions of them.

Michael, also from that same class, found both the drawing and the discussion useful. But he had a clear preference for the opportunity to talk about what he had sketched: "Talking about it was maybe more helpful than drawing. It helped me to develop my ideas further." Another student, Josett, found the pairing-up portion of this activity most useful. She found both the sketching and the discussion helpful, and she added these comments:

> It [the sketching] helped because I could break down my thinking process and see the steps I needed to take and the progress I was achieving with each step. It [the discussion] helped because my partner's input gave me another insight to how I could organize my essay. This [point of view] led me to see areas of my plan that would need reworking.

Josett's comments reflected three activities we did in that class session: sketching, sharing the JVRs and discussing them in pairs, and then more sharing and an open class discussion of several. For Josett, her partner's input was helpful. If time permits, that extra step of sharing in pairs may be critical for some writers.

Another student, Rida, commenting on this activity in a different class, checked the "Helped a lot" box for both questions, one on the helpfulness of JVR and the other on the discussion that followed. Her sketch, she said, depicted her need for better structure (see Figure 5.3).

Here is Rida's explanation of this sketch:

> The diagram on the left is how my paper is going in circles, like the ideas are revolving around each other but not exactly transitioning them well. The diagram on the right is how I would like to be, going from a consise [sic] like a thesis to broad, which is the argument and the base of the paper.

Rida's juxtaposed sketches here are simple, but together with her words they show that she is aware that her draft is "going in circles" and needs "transitioning." The view that she'd "like [it] to be structured" may not be a groundbreaking insight for academic writing. However, perhaps the fact that she herself made this critique of her own draft might help her pay more attention to structure and transitions as she revised her paper.

Figure 5.3. Rida's JVR of Her Current and Alternative Organization of Her Draft

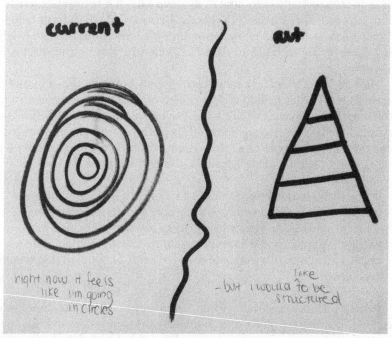

Two juxtaposed images. On the left, labeled "current," is a series of concentric circles. The sketcher has written below it: "Right now it feels like I'm going in circles." On the right, labeled "alt," is a pyramid divided by three parallel lines going horizontally through it. The sketcher has written below it: "—but I would like to be structured."

Possible Effects of JVRs on Revision

Rida's early draft, reflected in the JVR, was strung together with a few transitions and seven subheadings, even though the draft was only 10 pages long. In contrast, her final paper, which was 17 pages long, had an organized beginning where she provided a helpful overview of what would follow, and she introduced her sources with smooth signal phrases. The subheadings were gone, and paragraphs were linked instead with helpful transitions. I can't say for sure what helped her most in making those improvements on her project—my comments on her early draft, the JVR, or the class discussion. However, the changes she made are consistent with the plan she described in her explanation of her JVR. And here is what she wrote about the JVR on the survey that came later: "I found that before my visual diagram, I was confusing 'grammar' and 'writing' as one concept, when I wanted to express them as two very different concepts." About the discussion, she wrote: "I realized that my work had a lot of aspects to it that I wasn't including, how teaching writing is way more than just teaching grammar." So for Rida, the JVR and the class discussion contributed to conceptual insights, content enrichment, and major organizational improvements.

Alexa's juxtaposed plans (Figure 5.4) also illustrate a very different organizational pattern for a revised paper.

These two sketches contrast Alexa's current organization juxtaposed to an alternative one on her project on accessibility (regarding disability) in the classroom. She wrote: "I changed around the order of the parts of my paper, talking about the problems and lack of accessibility first and the examples

Figure 5.4. Alexa's JVR of Her Current Versus Possible Future Organization for Her Paper

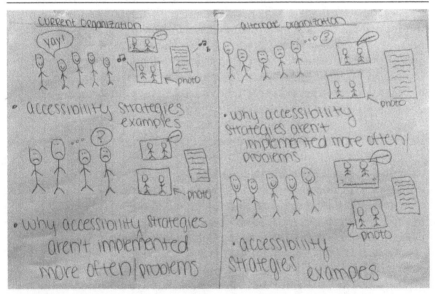

Two juxtaposed sketches. The left side, labeled "Current Organization," has five smiling stick figures saying "Yay!" as they look at two photographs, one of which has a musical note, and a letter that also has musical notes. The bullet below these figures says "accessibility strategies [and] examples." Below that are four other stick figures with unhappy faces and a question mark in a thought bubble as they look at two photos and a letter. The bullet below these figures says, "Why accessibility strategies aren't implemented more often/problems." The right side, labeled "Alternate Organization," begins with five stick figures with unhappy faces and a question mark in a thought bubble. They appear to be puzzled by the two photographs and the letter they are looking at. The bullet below it says, "Why accessibility strategies aren't implemented more often/problems." Below that are five happy stick figures looking at the same photos and letter. The bullet at the bottom says, "accessibility strategies [and] examples."

second." It is worth noting that in her original organization, she starts with apparently happy students enjoying examples of strategies to make texts accessible. Only later does she show dismayed students and start discussing "why accessibility strategies aren't implemented more often." In her new structure, by contrast, she begins with the concrete problem: that many students are dismayed by the lack of accessible materials. Then she gets into possible solutions to this problem. This second approach is not only more dramatic, potentially drawing and keeping more readers' attention. It is also more "academic," in a good way, beginning with a problem that needs to be solved, exploring the causes of the problem, and then suggesting ways to solve it.

When I compared Alexa's earlier draft with her final version, I could see that she added much material, but she actually did not reverse the order to discuss the lack of access first. She did not implement in her revision the radical organizational change she proposed in her JVR and in her description of it: to start with the problems of students not being accommodated. I cannot say why. Maybe she felt it was too much work to invest in a paper that was almost finished, or maybe she changed her mind about that proposed new beginning. Her juxtaposed structures, however, and the discussion that followed, might have helped other writers rethink how they could make their opening paragraphs more dramatic.

Different Effects on Different Students

As we have seen, some students found the sketching itself helpful in generating insights, while others did not. Some found the discussion more valuable than doing the actual drawing, and some found both useful. As can be seen in the mix of representative comments below, there was quite a range in how students reacted to the drawings and the discussions.

Regarding the JVRs:

Becca: "The problems that I faced would have to be solved through the endless process of writing and not really looking at the structure—though it was productive to have an overall picture of the problem simplified in my mind."

Kay: "Personally, visual representations help make dense concepts clear to me."

Erin: "It actually did help me think of a different way to organize my paper! (Though . . . I didn't use it.)"

Josett: "I had major problems with organization for my research paper so drawing out the structure and topics I wanted to hit was truly helpful as it opened my eyes to things I wasn't thinking about previously."

Tamra: I hadn't realized how disorganized I was until I was asked to sketch said disorganization. When having to draw or plot out my ideal paper, I was then thinking about what I'd like to read myself, less about what I actually wanted to produce. This helped me see my end goal in a new way."

Connor: "My sketch depicted an organizational problem I was encountering in my report. Using the metaphor of trying to pack everything you own into one suitcase, I conveyed the idea that I wanted to cover so many topics in one essay. The sketches helped me realize that it would be better to focus on a couple of topics in great detail, rather than trying to cram all my thoughts together."

Rejane: I like visual representation, using slides, drawings, pictures, cartoons, anything that can be useful in my teaching to provoke emotions, thinking and comprehension. As an ENL [English as a New Language] teacher we use a lot of media to help students experience the concepts we are trying to teach or to connect with their backgrounds.

Regarding the discussions:

Sara: "I preferred my original organizational sketch to my reworked sketch. However, through discussion, I got some great suggestions to consider for a future paper."

Erin: "I liked seeing what the rest of the class had come up with and felt like it could be really helpful to generate new ideas and perspectives."

Shauna: "I did not discuss my own visual, but I appreciated seeing other people's ideas and struggles because they gave me new perspectives/questions to apply to my own draft."

Connor: "After discussing my drawing, my conclusions were validated. Simply hearing someone else say that it would be better to dive deeper into a few topics than try to cover too wide of an area, made me feel like I could cut down and still produce good writing."

Tamra: "I enjoyed hearing about my peers' writing habits and strategies and liked learning about ways to organize a college paper—to be honest I don't know a professor who ever discussed essay formatting at the college level in depth, so it was nice to listen to and learn from my peers."

Studying these and other students' comments about this process on the surveys or in other conversations, I've learned how this intellectual exercise might be improved for use in future classes.

PROPOSED CHANGES TO THE PROCESS

First, I might have students create these organizational or problem-solving JVRs earlier in the process, or perhaps even twice: once earlier and once at this late date—a week before the project is due. In their comments about the comparative organization sketching, some students admitted that they already had a set plan. Matt, who checked "Not sure" for both Questions 6 and 7 regarding the usefulness of this class's drawing and discussion, wrote, "I just visually represented what I already knew I wanted to do, so not much came of it." Others were too far along in their draft to want to change the whole structure. They considered their projects virtually finished. Another student, Ella, checked "Didn't help at all" for Question 6 about doing the drawings. She wrote, "The fact that it did not help was not the fault of the visual representation. By the time we did that in class, I had a fairly complete draft of my paper, and I was being stubborn about different ways to organize it. I had organized it in a way I liked, and I was not about to change! :-)" Another student, Megan, commented that the visualization representation exercise didn't work well for her because she was almost finished: "Maybe I was too far along in my paper but it didn't feel like it helped too much in completing what needed to be done." For students like Ella and Megan, who get their work done ahead of most others, imagining an alternative structure at this point was absurd.

Second, I might address more directly the distaste some students may have for sketching. A few students honestly admitted that they worked exclusively through writing, which was true for me as well for several decades. This resistance to the visual is a common hurdle for instructors who wish to use JVRs as a teaching tool. In a complex study they did in 2011 with 3rd-graders in Budapest, Hungary, Csikos et al. (2012) wished to study the role visual representation could play in teaching students how to solve word problems. Interestingly, the researchers first had to convince their subjects that making drawings could help them solve word problems.

In major writing projects, we want students to learn to examine their own developing drafts, identify areas of improvement, and solve problems. Of course, we as instructors could read everyone's draft and respond individually to all of our students, providing suggestions for improvement regarding organization, structure, emphasis, and so on. This JVR activity does not preclude that time-consuming response. But this exercise, where students must focus on what they have so far and think abstractly about needed changes, can be productive on its own or in conjunction with teacher-heavy analysis and response. Students know their own drafts better than we do. Having them troubleshoot their own work so far and then propose changes for an improved draft can save time and promote fairly quick insights. The act of sketching itself is revelatory for some. When they juxtapose alternative organizational patterns or problems versus solutions, they literally see a way to improve their drafts. For others, seeing and hearing their classmates' issues, with input from the instructor, is a kind of productive crowd-sourcing and problem-solving event. It also can alert some writers to issues in their drafts that they didn't know they had. Spending a bit of class time to get students thinking in both focused and abstract ways about their work, through these JVRs and the discussions that follow the projections, is well worth the intellectual experimentation.

CHAPTER 6

Student Responses to Juxtaposed Visual Representations

So far, these chapters have provided examples of how JVRs were used to grapple with abstract ideas important to specific courses taken by future English teachers: teaching writing, studying English language(s), and analyzing approaches to choosing and teaching literature. Students used JVRs to contrast old and new terms in the field, to juxtapose different sides of controversies, and to help them reorganize their papers. The JVRs also helped us to explore racial prejudices toward speakers of Black English, as well as attitudes toward emergent bilingual students and toward students with disabilities.

The artistic quality of the sketches notwithstanding, we've seen how simple sketches can help to solidify the meaning of a concept necessary for advancement in a subject area. Occasionally some revealed students' misunderstanding of an important idea; others emerged as a useful counterpoint to those misunderstandings, providing a clear image or metaphor that helped to clarify needed distinctions between critical terms. The previous chapter provided examples of how some students found that the visuals themselves sparked insights, while others found that the discussions following the projections were more useful.

This chapter includes an analysis of all the surveys collected for this project, as well as some student commentary that can provide more insight into using JVRs as an intellectual exercise. Most answers come from the 54 students who granted written permission for me to use their visual representations and their answers to this survey, and who were also present in class the day we did the surveys or sent them to me after the class session. A few students neglected to answer the last two questions on the survey. This was because in some classes I distributed those two questions separately from the other questions so that the paper-related questions would be answered as close as possible to when they did the drawings of their paper organization. See the Appendix for the IRB-approved survey that I used with my classes.

ANALYZING SURVEY RESULTS

Students' answers to Question 1, which asked whether they had ever used visual representation in a college classroom before, confirmed my suspicion that most students had not done so. That is, they had not used sketches in a manner similar to ours, unless they counted the current class or a class they had taken with me previously in which we did JVRs. Fifteen of 54 students said that they had used visual representation only once, and 11 of those 15 said they had done so only with me. Only nine of 54 students said that they had used visual representation more than once, and four of those nine said they had done so only with me in a previous class. In retrospect, I should have worded the question more specifically, to ask whether they had done visual representations before this class with me, or before they had ever taken a class with me. One student explained briefly that they had done a visual exercise in a theater class, and one student counted doing a PowerPoint as a visual representation—neither of which I counted as a JVR. A couple of more students said they had done "something like that," but it was not clear that they had done what we were doing. Significantly, 24 students said they had never done a visual representation in a college classroom before. Therefore, not counting the students who had done them only with me (and not counting the theater exercise and the PowerPoint), only 9 of 54 students had done visual representation in a college classroom—only about 16% of students surveyed.

Also in retrospect, I might have asked specifically about "juxtaposed" visual representation, which might have brought that number and percentage down even lower. Therefore, somewhere between 80% and 90% of the students I taught in the semesters during which I conducted this research said that they had *not* used visual representation as a tool to promote learning, analysis, invention, or organization. Because these students are graduate or undergraduate English majors likely to teach or tutor English and/or writing on the high school or college level, it is important for them to experience learning strategies like this one that they can adapt to their future students' needs. It is likely that a number of their future students will process knowledge visually, and using JVRs to access or generate that knowledge is an inclusionary practice. Even students who prefer word-based intellectual tasks may benefit from the opportunity to think visually. As we will see, there are also emotionally supportive, affective advantages to producing, sharing, and discussing these JVRs.

Questions 2 and 3 asked whether students understood what they were being asked to do and why, when the task was first mentioned (Question 2) and then after they did a sample in class (Question 3). These two questions received the most consistent answers in all five classes. Only one person said that at first they did not understand why they were doing these visual representations, and that student said they were absent from class on the day the reasons were explained. Once they actually did the practice JVRs in class, 100% of the students said they understood what they were being asked to do and why. Knowing that many print-preferring English majors like myself might be skeptical of being asked to draw in a writing or English class, I made sure to tell students up front that I was asking them to sketch because it might help them process some ideas. Since we were taking valuable class time to do these sketches, I wanted students to take the activity seriously. I cannot say whether they understood the reasons for this activity in the same way I did, and my telling them the reasons up front might have influenced how they answered this question.

Questions 4 and 5 are similar in that both ask whether visual representation helped in understanding concepts studied in that class. Question 4 focuses on the actual creation of the visuals; Question 5 focuses on the oral and written discussion of the visuals as well as what students heard discussed in class. For Question 4, only two students selected "Didn't help at all," and four selected "Not sure." Significantly, 22 students checked "Helped a lot," and 26 checked "Helped a little," which meant that 48 out of 54 students, or over 88% of the class, said that they found that the visual representations helped them better understand concepts. The results were similar for Question 5, which asked about the effect of the written and oral discussions of the visuals. Only three students selected "Didn't help at all," and five students checked "Not sure." Twenty-four students picked "Helped a lot," and 21 picked "Helped a little." That meant that 45 out of 53 students who filled out that question, or 85%, said they found that writing about, discussing, and listening to discussions about the concepts represented in the visuals helped their understanding of this material.

The last two questions addressed whether contrasting the current organization pattern of their project drafts with a hypothetical alternative organization was useful (Question 6) and whether writing about those sketches, explaining them, or listening to explanations of them was useful (Question 7). Regarding the JVRs themselves, 13 of 52 students said it "helped a lot." One student, clearly not sure, gave half of her choice to "helped a little" and half of her choice to "not sure." There were 20½ students who said that it "helped a little." Answering "not sure" were 10½ students. Only six students said it "didn't help at all," while two other students explained that they were absent on the day we did the juxtaposed organizational patterns in class. To summarize, 33½ students, or about 64% of all students in the classes surveyed, said this activity helped "a lot" or "a little," and 10½ students, or about 20%, weren't sure. Only six students out of 52 said it "didn't help at all."

Question 7 asked about the written explanations and oral discussion that followed the 10-minute sketches we did in class. Saying it "helped a lot" were 14 students out of 53, or 26% of all students surveyed. And 24 students out of 53, or 45%, said it "helped a little." The "not sure" response had eight students out of 53, or 15%. Only five students out of 53, or 9%, said it "didn't help at all." (Two students wrote "not applicable" because they were absent for the discussion of the contrasted organizational patterns.)

To summarize, 38 students, or 71% of all students surveyed, said the writing about and discussing of the sketches helped either "a little" or "a lot." Interestingly, more students found the explanations of the sketches more helpful than the actual creation of the sketches, suggesting that if instructors do this activity, they certainly should invest time for students to explain their JVRs to the class and discuss what the sketches reveal. These numbers are consistent with the comments some students made about what helped them.

STUDENTS' COMMENTS

When asked about the effect of the discussion itself, one student, Corinne, said it helped a lot and wrote, "Hearing what other people are struggling with really helped me think about if I was also making the same errors. It encouraged me to check my paper out for those concerns." Josh, too, said the follow-up talk helped a little: "Discussion has also proven to be an invaluable tool over time. The more I say my ideas out loud, the more I tend to catch flaws myself. Having a peer provide extra insight is also always a plus." Vincent found the discussion more helpful than the drawing: "More than the visualization of my own, seeing other people's problems helped to solve my issues as well." The advantage of having students articulate their ideas when they explain and discuss their JVRs is consistent with what I learned by working in a writing center many years ago. Talk is an invention strategy. As people explain their ideas, they often generate other ideas, see more connections between them, or gain insights on how to solve a problem.

Another student, Hannah, was also not a fan of the visual part of the exercise: "It seemed like more of a task than a helping tool." But she also wrote this, pointing out something that never would have occurred to me: "Discussion of the work we did was helpful. It made me understand my professor and peers better." As I think about it now, after seeing Hannah's comment, I do think using JVRs and the subsequent discussion of them may help foster connection and community in the class. This may be because this brief, low-stakes exercise gets students' attention and pauses the business-as-usualness of the class. Then they get to see and hear about what their classmates produced. Since the JVRs are always all different, this sharing segment of the class is always interesting, intellectually stimulating, and, dare I say, fun. Anecdotally, I can report that when I introduce this task and demonstrate to students what I mean by a juxtaposed visual representation, I'm usually met with a stunned silence. It might be from overwhelming anxiety or bemused interest, but everyone is alert and paying attention. They also watch and listen intently as volunteers project their sketches and explain them. And Vincent pointed out another advantage to the explanatory discussion: "It brought up that I wasn't the only one having issues and that everyone runs into some trouble sometimes." It can be comforting, even empowering, for students to see they are not the only ones struggling with a challenging writing project.

What might these survey results and comments mean? First, some limitations: This was a small sample of students, all either upper-level English majors or master's students in English or English education. In addition, as with all surveys, the results reflect students' responses on the surveys, not necessarily an accurate view into their brains. In other words, students may have answered the way they did regarding the effects of the sketches because they thought it was what I wanted to hear. Or, alternatively, students may have said the sketches did not help them because they hate sketching and don't want to encourage me to use more of them. The results, therefore, should be read with those possibilities in mind.

CONCLUSION

The generally strong positive reaction of these students to using JVRs is significant. These surveys and comments also support cross-disciplinary findings on the effectiveness of the picture-superiority effect (Childers & Houston, 1984), multisensory pathways, and active learning. They reinforce how thinking is influenced by emotion, which contemporary neurologists have documented, and ancient rhetoricians taught as pathos, as described in Chapter 2. JVRs can force instructors and students alike to identify and review critical concepts in the course. As we've seen from the examples in Chapter 3, the JVRs also can reveal previously undiagnosed misunderstandings and help to clarify terms.

What's more, sketching JVRs, describing them, and discussing them in class can help students explore the long-term implications of contrasting concepts or controversies in education. As we've seen in Chapter 5, JVRs also can help students with deep revision and reorganization of their developing written projects. The high percentage of students who said the sketches and/or discussions of them were generally helpful to them in understanding concepts or reorganizing their papers makes this activity something worth exploring further in our classes.

Survey—Students' Views on Using Juxtaposed Visual Representations

Below is the IRB-approved survey that I used with my classes. (I've eliminated some of the white space that appeared on the original survey and was included for students who wished to explain their answers.)

This Appendix is available for free as a printable PDF file on the TC Press website. Click on the "Appendix: Survey" tab on the book's product page at https://www.tcpress.com/drawing-conclusions-9780807764923

SURVEY/QUESTIONNAIRE
VISUAL REPRESENTATION IN ENGLISH OR WRITING CLASSES

Name:

1. Have you ever used visual representation in a college classroom before? Please circle.

    Yes, once

    Yes, more than once

    No, but something like that

    Never

    If yes, where and when?

    Explain if you'd like to:

2. **When the professor first introduced visual representation in this class, to what extent did you understand what you were being asked to do and why?**

    Yes, got the what and why

    Yes, got the what but not why

    Had an inkling

    Not a clue

    Explain if you'd like to:

3. **After using visual representation more than once in class and discussing it or writing about it (or hearing others discuss it), to what extent did you understand what you were being asked to do and why?**

    Yes, got the what and why

    Yes, got the what but not why

    Had an inkling

    Not a clue

    Explain if you'd like to:

4. **After creating a visual representation to sketch out concepts in class reading(s) or lessons, to what extent did the creation of your visual representation help you better understand the concepts?**

    Helped a lot

    Helped a little

    Not sure

    Didn't help at all

    Explain if you'd like to:

5. After discussing your visual representation or writing about it (or hearing others discuss it), to what extent did you understand, to what extent did the creation of your visual representation help you better understand the concepts?

   Helped a lot

   Helped a little

   Not sure

   Didn't help at all

   Explain if you'd like to:

6. After creating a visual representation to sketch out ideas or possible organizational patterns in your written draft, to what extent did the creation of your visual representation give you productive insights about your work?

   Helped a lot

   Helped a little

   Not sure

   Didn't help at all

   Explain if you'd like to:

7. After discussing your visual representation of your organizational patterns in your drafts or writing about it (or hearing others discuss it), to what extent did this strategy give you productive insights about your work?

   Helped a lot

   Helped a little

   Not sure

   Didn't help at all

   Explain if you'd like to:

References

Albers, P., Holbrook, T., & Flint, A. (Eds.). (2013). *New methods in literacy research.* Routledge.

Anson, C. M. (2000). Response and the social construction of error. *Assessing Writing, 7*(1), 5–21. https://doi.org/10.1016/s1075-2935(00)00015-5

Anson, I. G., & Anson, C. M. (2017). Assessing peer and instructor response to writing: A corpus analysis from an expert survey. *Assessing Writing, 33,* 12–24. https://doi.org/10.1016/j.asw.2017.03.001

Arnold, M. (1869). *Culture & anarchy: An essay in political and social criticism.* Smith, Elder & Company.

Baker-Bell, A. (2020). *Linguistic justice: Black language, literacy, identity, and pedagogy.* Routledge.

Bambara, T. C. (1974). On the issue of Black English. *Confrontation: A Journal of Third World Literature, 1*(3), 103–117.

Baugh, A. C., & Cable, T. (2002). *A history of the English language* (5th ed.). Routledge.

Britton, J. (1982). *Prospect and retrospect: Selected essays of James Britton* (G. Pradl, Ed.). Heinemann.

Calhoon-Dillahunt, C., & Forrest, D. (2013). Conversing in marginal spaces: Developmental writers' responses to teacher comments. *Teaching English in the Two-Year College, 40*(3), 230–247.

Canagarajah, A. S. (2006). The place of world Englishes in composition: Pluralization continued. *College Composition and Communication, 57*(4), 586–619.

Childers, T. L., & Houston, M. J. (1984). Conditions for a picture-superiority effect on consumer memory. *Journal of Consumer Research, 11*(2), 643–654. https://www.jstor.org/stable/2488971

Clark, C., & Ivanic, R. (1997). *The politics of writing.* Routledge.

Clore, G., & Gasper, K. (2000). Feeling is believing: Some affective influences on belief. In N. H. Frijda, A. S. R. Mansead, & S. Bem (Eds.), *Emotions and beliefs: How do emotions influence beliefs?* (pp. 10–44). Cambridge University Press. https://www.researchgate.net/publication/238232607_Feeling_is_Believing_Some_Affective_Influences_on_Belief

Cook, A., & Frey, S. (2019). Reading in time: Cognitive dynamics and the literary experience of Shakespeare. In L. Magnusson & D. Schalkwyk (Eds.), *The Cambridge companion to Shakespeare's language* (pp. 189–204). Cambridge University Press. https://doi.org/10.1017/9781316443668.011

Crowley, S. (2006). *Toward a civil discourse: Rhetoric and fundamentalism.* University of Pittsburgh Press. https://www.jstor.org/stable/j.ctt5hjng7

Crowley, S., & Hawhee, D. (1998). *Ancient rhetorics for contemporary students.* Longman.

Csikos, C., Szitányi, J., & Kelemen, R. (2012). The effects of using drawings in developing young children's mathematical word problem solving: A design experiment with third-grade Hungarian students. *Educational Studies in Mathematics, 81,* 47–65. https://doi.org/10.1007/s10649-011-9360-z

Daiker, D. (1989). Learning to praise. In C. M. Anson (Ed.), *Writing and response* (pp. 103–113). National Council of Teachers of English.

Damasio, A. R., Everitt, B. J., & Bishop, D. (1996). The somatic marker hypothesis and the possible functions of the prefrontal cortex. *Philosophical Transactions: Biological Sciences, 351*(1346), 1413–1420. https://www.jstor.org/stable/3069187

Dean, D. (2003). Framing texts: New strategies for student writers. *Voices from the Middle, 11*(2), 32–35.

Diederich, P. (1963). In praise of praise. *NEA Journal, 52,* 58–59.

Dolmage, J. T. (2017). *Academic ableism: Disability and higher education.* University of Michigan Press.

Dunn, P. A. (2001). *Talking, sketching, moving: Multiple literacies in the teaching of writing.* Boynton/Cook Heinemann.

Dunn, P. A. (2015). *Disabling characters: Representations of disability in young adult literature.* Peter Lang.

Dunn, P. A., & De Mers, K. D. (2002). Reversing notions of disability and accommodation: Embracing universal design in writing pedagogy and web space. *Kairos: Rhetoric, Technology, Pedagogy, 7*(1). http://kairos.technorhetoric.net/7.1/binder2.html?coverweb/dunn_demers/index.html

Dunn, P. A., & Lindblom, K. (2011). *Grammar rants: How a backstage tour of writing complaints can help students make informed, savvy choices about their writing.* Boynton/Cook Heinemann.

Ebarvia, T., Parker, K. N., German, L., & J. E. Torres. (n.d.). #DisruptTexts (website and blog). https://disrupttexts.org/

Fahnestock, J., & Secor, M. (1991). The rhetoric of literary criticism. In C. Bazerman & J. Paradis (Eds.), *Textual dynamics of the professions* (pp. 74–96). University of Wisconsin Press.

Fauconnier, G., & Turner, M. (2008). Rethinking metaphor. In R. Gibbs (Ed.), *Cambridge handbook of metaphor and thought* (pp. 53–66). Cambridge University Press.

Freire, P. (1993). *Education for critical consciousness.* Continuum.

Garner, B. A. (2009). *Garner's modern American usage* (3rd ed.). Oxford University Press.

Gates, H. L. (1994). Canon-formation, literary history, and the Afro-American tradition. In D. H. Richter (Ed.), *Falling into theory: Conflicting views on reading literature* (pp. 174–182). St. Martin's Press. (Reprinted from *Afro-American literary studies in the 1990s,* pp. 14–39, by H. A. Baker, Jr., & P. Redmond, Eds., 1989, University of Chicago Press)

Gilyard, K. (2000). Literacy, identity, imagination, flight. *College Composition and Communication, 52*(2), 260–272. https://www.jstor.org/stable/358496

Guerra, J. C. (2012). *From code-segregation to code-switching to code-meshing: Finding deliverance from deficit thinking through language awareness and performance* [Plenary address, December 2011]. Literacy Research Association Conference, Jacksonville, FL, United States.

Hadjioannou, X., & Hutchinson, M. (2014). Fostering awareness through transmediation: Preparing pre-service teachers for critical engagement with multicultural literature. *International Journal of Multicultural Education, 16*(1), 1–20. https://ijme-journal.org/index.php/ijme/article/view/692

Hallman, H. (2009). Authentic, dialogic writing: The case of a letter to the editor. *English Journal, 98*(5), 43–47.

Herrnstein Smith, B. (1997). *Belief and resistance: Dynamics of contemporary intellectual controversy.* Harvard University Press.

Hillocks, G., Jr. (1984). What works in teaching composition: A meta-analysis of experimental treatment studies. *American Journal of Education, 93*(1), 133–170. https://www.jstor.org/stable/1085093

Kirkland, D. E., & Jackson, A. (2008). Beyond the silence: Instructional approaches and students' attitudes. In J. Scott, D. Y. Straker, & L. Katz (Eds.), *Affirming students' rights to their own language: Bridging educational policies and language/language arts teaching practices* (pp. 160–180). National Council of Teachers of English; Routledge.

Lakoff, G., & Johnson, M. (1980). *Metaphors we live by.* University of Chicago Press.

LeMoine, N. R. (2001). Language variation and literacy acquisition in African American students. In J. Harris, A. G. Kamki, & K. E. Pollock (Eds.), *Literacy in African American communities* (pp. 169–194). Erlbaum.

Lindblom, K. L. (2015). School writing vs. authentic writing. *Teachers, Profs, Parents: Writers Who Care.* https://writerswhocare.wordpress.com/2015/07/27/school-writing-vs-authentic-writing/

Lindblom, K. L., & Christenbury, L. (2018). *Continuing the journey 2: Becoming a better teacher of authentic writing.* National Council of Teachers of English.

Lippi-Green, R. (2012). *English with an accent: Language, ideology, and discrimination in the United States* (2nd ed.). Routledge.

Mack, N. (2013). Colorful revision: Color-coded comments connected to instruction. *Teaching English in the Two-Year College, 40*(3), 248–256. http://www.ncte.org/journals/tetyc/issues/v40-3

McWhorter, J. (2008). *Our magnificent bastard tongue: The untold history of English.* Penguin Random House.

Meyer, J., & Land, R. (2003). *Threshold concepts and troublesome knowledge: Linkages to ways of thinking and practising within the disciplines.* Occasional Report 4, Enhancing teaching-learning environments in undergraduate courses project. University of Edinburgh. https://www.colorado.edu/ftep/sites/default/files/attached-files/meyer_and_land_-_threshold_concepts.pdf

Mitchell, D., & Snyder, S. (2000). *Narrative prosthesis: Disability and the dependencies of discourse.* University of Michigan Press.

New London Group. (1996). A pedagogy of multiliteracies: Designing social futures. *Harvard Educational Review, 66*(1), 60–93. https://doi.org/10.17763/haer.66.1.17370n67v22j160u

NYSED. (2017). New York State Next Generation English Language Arts Learning Standards, p. 123. http://www.nysed.gov/common/nysed/files/programs/curriculum-instruction/nys-next-generation-ela-standards.pdf

Paris, D. (2012). Culturally sustaining pedagogy: A needed change in stance, terminology, and practice. *Educational Researcher, 41*(3), 93–97.

Perkins, D. (1999). The many faces of constructivism. *Educational Leadership, 57*(3), 6–11.

Portillo, A. (2013). Indigenous-centered pedagogies: Strategies for teaching Native American literature and culture. *The CEA Forum, 42*(1), 155–178.

Richter, D. H. (1994). *Falling into theory: Conflicting views on reading literature.* St. Martin's Press.

Robb, L. (2010). *Teaching middle school writers: What every English teacher needs to know.* Heinemann.

Semali, L. (2002). Transmediation: Why study the semiotics of representation? In L. Semali (Ed.), *Transmediation in the classroom: A semiotics-based media literacy framework* (pp. 1–20). Peter Lang.

Shor, I. (1999). What is critical literacy? *Journal of Pedagogy, Pluralism and Practice, 1*(4). https://digitalcommons.lesley.edu/jppp/vol1/iss4/2

Siegel, M. (1995). More than words: The generative power of transmediation for learning. *Canadian Journal of Education, 20*(4), 455–475. https://doi.org/10.2307/1495082

Smitherman, G. (2012, September). Handlin our (unfinished) bidness. *The Council Chronicle,* pp. 24–25.

Sousanis, N. (2015). *Unflattening.* Harvard University Press.

Walsh, L. (2017). Visual invention and the composition of scientific research graphics: A topological approach. *Written Communication, 35*(1), 3–31.

Wheeler, R. S., & Swords, R. (2006). *Code-switching: Teaching standard English in urban classrooms.* National Council of Teachers of English.

Wiggans, G. (2009). Real-world writing: Making purpose and audience matter. *English Journal, 98*(5), 29–37.

Williams, J. (1981). The phenomenology of error. *College Composition and Communication, 32*(2), 152–168. https://www.jstor.org/stable/356689

Young, V. A., Barrett, R., Young-Rivera, Y-S, & Lovejoy, K. B. (2014). *Other people's English: Code-meshing, code-switching, and African American literacy.* Teachers College Press.

Index

About the Author

Patricia A. Dunn is professor of English at Stony Brook University in New York, where she teaches future and current English teachers and writing instructors. Her books include *Learning Re-Abled* (1995); *Talking, Sketching, Moving* (2001); *Grammar Rants* (2011, co-written with Ken Lindblom), which is a critique of published complaints about "grammar" and how to use those critiques to empower students; and *Disabling Characters: Representations of Disability in Young Adult Literature* (2015).